# HOW

# PARLIAMENT

# WORKS

# Acknowledgements

This book owes so much to so many people that it is impossible to adequately acknowledge the various sources from which help was received. Special thanks, however, must be extended to Richard Paré, Parliamentary Librarian; The Public Information Office; Mark Audcent; Deborah Palumbo and André Reny. In addition, I am indebted to Francine Bellanger from Government House, Hélène Papineau from Elections Canada and to photographers Peter Sibbald and Michelle Kittelberg.

For profiles of individual Parliamentarians, see the bilingual *The Canadian Parliamentary Handbook/Répertoire Parlementaire Canadien.* Annual editions available from Borealis Press Ltd., from 1982

John Bejermi

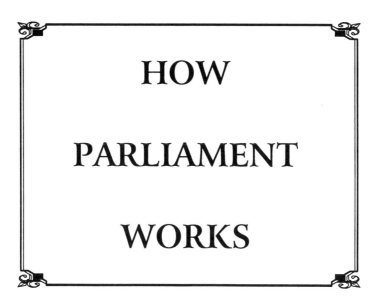

# HOW

# PARLIAMENT

# WORKS

Borealis Press
Ottawa, Canada
1996

4th edition 1996, 1st edition 1980, 2nd edition 1985, 3rd edition 1990

Borealis Press Limited
9 Ashburn Drive
Ottawa, Ontario, Canada K2E 6N4

Canadian Cataloguing in Publication Data

Bejermi, John, 1952-
How Parliament works : 4th ed.

ISBN 0-88887-139-2 (bound)
ISBN 0-88887-141-4 (pbk.)

1. Canada. Parliament. I. Title.

JL136.B43 1996      328.71'07      C96-900590-3

# Table of Contents

# *Preface*

When I began researching this fourth edition, I quickly realized the amount of political turmoil which has affected many governments throughout the world since the publication of my first edition in 1980. Canadians should feel fortunate and proud to live in a country where a parliamentary system exists: a system enabling its citizens, at each general election, to freely choose the party which will, through lively parliamentary debate, ensure that democracy continues.

The purpose of this edition is to provide Canadians with an opportunity to understand how their Parliament works. My objective is to bring Parliament closer to Canadians through a presentation that may be understood by both scholars and students. It is not my intent to duplicate or replace numerous authorities available on our parliamentary system of government, but merely to complement them.

It is my view that when people understand their system of government, not only in form but also in substance, they become more interested and involved in the political process. This interest and involvement enables them to challenge and demand more from their appointed and elected parliamentarians. This awareness, in my opinion, is crucial to maintaining our national unity.

*1996*                                                                 *John Bejermi*

*The Centre Block with the constantly burning Centennial Flame in foreground. All of Canada's Provincial crests are handsomely reproduced on centrepiece.*

# Chapter 1

# Parliamentary Government
# in a Canadian Context

As we approach the next century, it is difficult not to reflect upon the interesting political events that have occurred during the last decade. Some of these historic events have occurred, not only in Canada, but throughout the world.

Internationally, we have witnessed historic changes, which included the tearing down of the Berlin Wall, the break-up of the Soviet Union, a Peace Treaty and a famous hand shake between two longtime enemies—Israel and the PLO (Palestine Liberation Organization).

Domestically, we have seen the rise of the Progressive Conservative Party where, under Mr. Brian Mulroney's leadership, the Conservatives elected two successive majority governments. We have also witnessed that Party's devastating defeat in the 1993 general election when, under Kim Campbell's leadership, it lost official recognition as a party in the House of Commons— only two Members were elected. Canadians also sent a strong message to the New Democratic Party, of which only nine Members were elected to the House of Commons during the 1993 general election. As a result, it too did not qualify as an official Party in the House of Commons.

Canadians observed the birth of two new political parties, which elected Members to the House of Commons—the Reform Party and the Bloc Québécois, a Quebec sovereignist Party that became "Her Majesty's Official Opposition" after the 1993 general election.

These changes, within Canadian politics, serve as a useful reminder that Canadian voters are prepared, if necessary, to elect new political parties in order that their interests be adequately protected. These changes reinforce the fact that politicians will be held accountable and that the people will no longer tolerate those who fail to deliver on their election promises. Today, more and more Canadians are anxious to participate in the political process and, as such, wish to better understand their system of government. Indeed, it is only through such an understanding that they may demand that the government

1

operate more effectively. These recent events are clear evidence that "democracy" is alive in Canada today. In fact, it is safe to say that democracy is considered the basis upon which the Canadian political system is built.

Canada is well-respected internationally and serves as a model for many countries of the world seeking democracy. During the last decade, we have witnessed those living in countries under communism or dictatorial rule who have either risked or lost their lives in the name of democracy.

"Democracy" has its roots in the Greek word "*demokratia*," meaning "people-power." It is on behalf of the people that power is exercised. One might ask, "What power?" The power of all citizens to freely choose their government. This type of government rests on the will of the people. It must, at all times, be responsive to that will; it exists mainly to serve the citizens of the country and to provide them with a satisfactory quality of life.

## *Principle Features*

Two principle features of Canada's parliamentary system of government are:

1. it is representative and responsible; and
2. it is a democratic federation.

Each of these features will be examined in turn.

### *Representative and Responsible*

What does it mean to say that our system is "representative and responsible"? Essentially, it means that there is a close relationship between the executive and legislative branches of government—the executive branch being represented by the Cabinet and the legislative branch consisting of Parliament itself.

Thus, the Cabinet which initiates policy and oversees the enforcement of the law, must work in harmony with, and be responsive to, the representative body—Parliament. Parliament, in turn, enacts the laws and exercises a function of public scrutiny and supervision over the policy decisions of the executive.

This system can only work effectively if the Prime Minister and members of the Cabinet are represented in Parliament. They must, at all times, be responsible to the House of Commons, and if they cannot maintain the support of that House, then they must resign or seek a dissolution of Parliament and resolve the situation through an election.

## Democratic Federation

The expression "democratic federation" simply means that Canada is a democracy—people have the power to change governments freely and may criticize their politicians without risk of punishment.

Canada is also a federation, which means that the powers of government are distributed between a central or federal government, on the one hand, and ten provincial governments on the other.[1] What are these powers? The issuance of money, for example, is a federal power, while education is a provincial power. This system was adopted in 1867, when Ontario, Quebec, New Brunswick and Nova Scotia joined together to form one country called Canada. The original act of union was called the *British North America Act, 1867*. It was renamed the *Constitution Act, 1867*. This Act formally established a federal system of government and it also formally provided that the monarch of Great Britain was to be the chief executive and head of state of Canada.

The *Constitution Act, 1867* also established one Parliament for Canada consisting of the Queen, an Upper House called the Senate, and the House of Commons. The composition of the House of Commons was to be established on the basis of representation by population, while the principle underlying the composition of the Senate was to be that of regional representation. Each was to have an equal voice in the enactment of Legislation.

This federal system meant that legislative jurisdiction over Canada was to be divided between the federal Parliament and each of the provincial legislatures. The federal Parliament was given the power "to make laws for the peace, order and good government of Canada," with the exception of those "classes of subjects ... assigned exclusively to the legislatures of the provinces."

Examples of some of these exclusive provincial powers are the following: direct taxation within the province for provincial purposes; natural resources belonging to the province; the establishment of charitable and municipal institutions; local works and undertakings (with certain exceptions); the incorporation of provincial companies; the solemnization of marriage; property and civil

---

[1] The two territorial governments also hold certain powers within the federation, although they are not as extensive as those held by the provinces.

3

rights in the province; the establishment of courts and the administration of justice; fines and penalties for the non-observance of provincial laws; and generally all matters of a merely local or private nature in the province. Education is also a matter of exclusive provincial jurisdiction, subject to certain rights of the Protestant and Roman Catholic minorities in any province.

Under the *Constitution Act, 1867,* any power not exclusively identified as a provincial power belongs to the federal Parliament. Examples of federal powers are set out in the Constitution and include the following: public debt and property; the regulation of trade and commerce; unemployment insurance; the raising of money by any mode or system of taxation; the borrowing of money on the public credit; postal service; the census and statistics; national defence; navigation and shipping; fisheries; currency and carriage; banking; interest; bills of exchange; bankruptcy; patents; copyrights; Indian lands; weights and measures; marriage and divorce; and the criminal law, except the constitution of the courts but including procedure in criminal matters.

As stated in a Senate committee report[1], this division of powers between the two levels of government represented in 1867, "a compromise between the unitary system of government then in existence in Great Britain and the type of federalism adopted in the United States." The Fathers of Confederation "became convinced that British North America needed a more centralized federalism than the U.S. Model." The report quotes Sir John A. MacDonald's description of this compromise in the following terms:

> We have given to the General Legislature all the great subjects of Legislation. We have conferred on them, not only specifically and in detail, all the powers which are incident to sovereignty but we have expressly declared that all subjects not distinctly and exclusively conferred upon the local governments and local legislatures shall be conferred upon the General Government and Legislature. We have thus avoided that great source of weakness which has been the cause of disruptions of the United States.

Thus, as the report states, "the federal government was given a dominant role within Canadian federalism. It received the main responsibilities that the state was expected to exercise at that time. Moreover, it was allotted

---

[1] *Report on Certain Aspects of the Canadian Constitution,* A report to the Senate of Canada, The Standing Senate Committee on Legal and Constitutional Affairs, Minister of Supply and Services Canada, November 1980, p. 3.

jurisdiction over all matters not specifically given to the provincial legislatures."

Although the powers described in the Constitution still exist today, discussions have been ongoing for years between the federal and provincial governments to determine the extent of the allocation of these powers to each level of government within the confines of the Constitution. Some subjects that were of minor importance when the Constitution was written are today of vital importance. Some of the provincial responsibilities have expanded, while the federal government has, for example, more substantial taxing powers and, therefore, a more substantial treasury. Frequent meetings between the two levels of government, known as federal-provincial conferences, have taken place over the years to try to work out problems of jurisdiction between the two legislative authorities.

The preamble of the Canadian Constitution states that Canada is to have a constitution "similar in principle to that of the United Kingdom." This means that, like the British Constitution, which is unwritten, much of what is part of the Canadian Constitution is also unwritten. For example, the Cabinet, the Prime Minister, responsible government, political parties, and federal-provincial conferences are all part of the system of government in Canada although they are not explicitly mentioned in the Constitution.

One basic constitutional difference between the systems of government in Canada and Great Britain is that Great Britain, like France and Italy, has a unitary system of government. This means that it has only one government and is called a unitary state; by contrast, Canada has a federal system of government and for this reason, as explained earlier, it is called a federation.

A federation has been defined as "the formation of a political unity with a central government, by a number of separate member states, each of which retains control of its own internal affairs." What characterizes a federation, as one government publication explains, "is that two sovereign governments with complementary jurisdiction co-exist in a given area."[1]

The common feature between the systems of government in Canada and Great Britain is, of course, the institution of Parliament. The word "Parliament" has its origin in the French word "parler," meaning "to speak or discuss." Parliament, then, is a meeting place where the representatives of the people can speak, discuss, criticize, argue and express their opinions publicly

---

[1] *Confederation, Unitary system, Federation*, Minister of Supply and Services Canada, 1982, p. 3.

on all matters of state. In Canada, therefore, we have a system called parliamentary government.

### *Parliamentary Government Defined*

Parliamentary Government means that government is carried out in the name of the Queen, by and with the advice and consent of the Senate and House of Commons. It also means that the ministers of the Queen's Privy Council, who form the Cabinet, should have seats in the House of Commons or in the Senate and must at all times retain the support of the majority of the members of the House of Commons in order to stay in office. It is for this reason that the expressions "responsible government" and "Cabinet government" are sometimes used to describe the Canadian system.

As indicated earlier, the Constitution provides for "the executive government of and over Canada" to be "vested in the Queen." Thus the Queen is head of state and symbolizes Canada's status as a "constitutional monarchy," a less commonly used term to describe Canada. The Queen ordinarily acts through the Governor General, who is appointed by the Queen, on the advice of the Prime Minister.

# HOUSE OF COMMONS
# CHAMBRE DES COMMUNES
# CANADA

### THE ARMS OF CANADA

The Arms of Canada are the Arms of the Sovereign; they signify national sovereignty or ownership. They are used in Canada on federal government possessions such as buildings, official seals, money, passports, proclamations, publications, etc., as well as rank badges of some members of the Canadian Forces. The present design of the Arms of Canada was approved in 1994 and shows a ribbon behind the shield with the motto of the Order of Canada.

# Chapter 2

## Our Constitution

### Origins

In Canada, there is no one document comparable to the American Constitution. The *British North America Act, 1867* (B.N.A. Act), which was renamed the *Constitution Act, 1867* in 1982, most closely resembles such a document. The *B.N.A. Act* established the new Dominion of Canada by merging three of the colonies of British North America and by providing the framework for the admission of all the other British North American colonies and territories. The *B.N.A. Act* set out the rules of federalism. This involved allocating certain powers to the federal Parliament and others to the provincial Legislatures.

The *B.N.A. Act* in no way created an independent country. In fact, independence from the United Kingdom was not even contemplated by the fathers of Confederation. Since the *B.N.A. Act* was an Act of the British Parliament, Canada had to turn to Britain each time it wanted to amend the *Act*. Over the years, the British Parliament, at the request of the Canadian government, made more than twenty amendments to the Constitution. Despite the fact that Canada did not have complete independence with the *B.N.A. Act*, it had achieved responsible government and a large measure of self-government in local matters.

With time, however, it became apparent to Canadians that the Constitution would have to be adapted in order to meet the changing needs of Canadians. To this end, Canadian Prime Ministers and provincial premiers had discussed the issue of Canadian independence from the United Kingdom for over fifty years at several federal-provincial conferences. Not surprisingly, they could not agree on a formula that would allow constitutional changes to be made in Canada.

# Patriation

In the fall of 1980, the federal government, with the support of the provinces of Ontario and New Brunswick, proposed a constitutional package to Parliament. A Special Joint Committee of the Senate and the House of Commons was established to discuss changes to the Constitution. Hundreds of groups and individuals from all across Canada made submissions to the Committee. These resulted in over seventy substantive changes to the government's original proposal.

Parliament debated the issue but, on September 28, 1981, the Supreme Court of Canada ruled that, while Parliament could legally proceed unilaterally, such an action would not be in accordance with a "convention" requiring a "substantial measure of provincial consent." As a result of this ruling, the Prime Minister and provincial premiers resumed negotiations. These negotiations resulted in the November 5, 1981 historic agreement with the federal government and the nine provincial governments. The province of Quebec, however, withheld its consent.

This agreement was the basis for the presentation of a new resolution to Parliament. The new resolution was passed by the House of Commons and the Senate in December, 1981 and it formed the basis of a Joint Address to the Queen requesting that the United Kingdom Parliament pass the *Canada Act.* The United Kingdom Parliament finally approved the bill on March 25, 1982, and, on March 29, 1982, the *Canada Act* received royal assent in Great Britain. This set the stage for "patriation" through proclamation in Canada of the *Constitution Act, 1982* (see Appendix 1).

The *Canada Act* accomplished two things. First, it ended Great Britain's power to legislate for Canada by transferring the authority to do so from Great Britain to Canada, although Canada's ties to the United Kingdom have been preserved through formal recognition of the Queen. Second, it included in the Constitution of Canada the *Constitution Act, 1982,* which contains a Charter of Rights and Freedoms.

## Canada's Modern Constitution[1]

The Canadian Constitution has four principal features. Two are as old as Confederation itself and are to be found in the *Constitution Act, 1867.* The

---

[1] This section has been prepared by Mark Audcent.

other two are new and are found in the *Constitution Act, 1982.*
The *Constitution Act, 1867* remains the cornerstone of the Constitution of Canada. The following two features are embedded within it:

*1. Constitutional monarchy and parliamentary democracy*

First, the 1867 Act makes Canada both a constitutional monarchy and a parliamentary democracy. It provides, in general terms, that Canada is to have a Constitution similar in principle to that of the United Kingdom. It then legislates many of the specifics of that system of government, such as providing for an executive government and for a Parliament composed of the Senate and the House of Commons.

*2. Confederation with a division of powers*

Second, the 1867 Act makes Canada a confederation by legislating a union and then explicitly providing for the division of powers between the Parliament of Canada and the Legislatures of the Provinces. The division of powers is found in sections 91 and 92 of the Act.

The Constitution Act, 1982 is a new model built on the old structure. Its two central features are the following:

A. Self-governing with a constitutional amending formula

First, the 1982 Act nationalizes (patriates) the Constitution. It provides for different formulas to amend different matters in the Constitution. What all these formulas have in common is that they are all decided and implemented by Canadians.

The most important constitutional amendments require the unanimous consent of the Senate, the House of Commons and every provincial Legislature. Most amendments can be passed under the general formula, which requires the consent of the Senate, the House of Commons and seven legislatures representing 50% of the population. Matters considered less important or of a local nature may require a less stringent formula, or may be dealt with by Parliament or a provincial Legislature acting alone.

Having provided Canada with an in-house mechanism to amend its Constitution in the future, the United Kingdom was in a position to relinquish its power to legislate amendments for Canadians.

B. The Canadian Charter of Rights and Freedoms

Second, the 1982 Act contains the *Canadian Charter of Rights and Freedoms* (see Appendix 2). The Charter guarantees a set of civil liberties that Canadian society considers to be so fundamental that they require protection from state action. The Charter has generated a great deal of interest among Canadians. In fact, most Canadians recognize that the Charter exists to protect their rights, although they may not necessarily understand the exact nature of those rights.

Many of the rights and freedoms found in the Charter are expressed in sweeping terms, which can result in uncertainty as to the extent of the protection they were intended to provide. The language used is very broad in order to express general principles. For example, the Charter provides that "every citizen has the right to vote in an election," but under the law, youth (individuals under 18 years of age) are not entitled to vote.

Another example of the broad language used in the Charter is the provision that "everyone has the right to life, liberty and security of the person." Despite this protection, people are imprisoned on a daily basis. Under the Charter, "every individual has the right to the equal protection and equal benefit of the law without discrimination", yet statistics indicate that women and children in our society are disproportionately below the poverty line.

The limits and extent of these rights have been left to be determined by the courts and, while some of the provisions of the Charter have already been judicially considered, many have yet to be clarified. Inevitably, how these provisions are interpreted will largely depend on the value systems—social, economic and political—of the individual judges called upon to decide Charter cases.

11

*Fathers of Confederation*

The picture above shows the participants to the historic Quebec Conference in 1864 as depicted by artist Rex Woods, which led to the Union of Canada. This was accomplished through the creation of the *British North America Act, 1867*, known today as the *Constitution Act, 1867*. As a result of their actions, these representatives are referred to as the "Fathers of Confederation."

# *Key to Painting of Fathers of Confederation*

1. Hewitt Bernard, Secretary
2. William H. Steeves, N.-B.
3. Edward Whelan, P. E. I.
4. William A. Henry, N. S.
5. Charles Fisher, N. B.
6. John Hamilton Gray, P. E. I.
7. Edward Palmer, P. E. I.
8. George H. Coles, P. E. I.
9. S. Leonard Tilley, N. B.
10. Frederic B. T. Carter, Nfld.
11. Jean Charles Chapais, Canada
12. J. Ambrose Shea, Nfld.
13. Edward B. Chandler, N. B.
14. Alexander Campbell, Canada
15. Adams G. Archibald, N. S.
16. Hector L. Langevin, Canada East
17. John A. Macdonald, Canada West
18. George Etienne Cartier, Canada East
19. Sir Etienne P. Taché, Canada
20. George Brown, Canada
21. T. Heath Haviland, P. E. I.
22. Alexander T. Galt, Canada
23. Peter Mitchell, N. B.
24. James Cockburn, Canada West
25. Oliver Mowat, Canada
26. Robert B. Dickey, N. S.
27. Dr. Charles Tupper, N. S.
28. John Hamilton Gray, N. B.
29. William H. Pope, P. E. I.
30. William McDougall, Canada
31. Thomas D'Arcy McGee, Canada
32. Andrew A. Macdonald, P. E. I.
33. Jonathan McCully, N. S.
34. John M. Johnson, N. B.
35. Robert D. Wilmot, N. B.
36. William P. Howland, Canada
37. John W. Ritchie, N. S.
38. Tribute to Robert Harris, CMG, RCA

*The Governor General in the Senate Chamber addressing Parliament.*

# Chapter 3

# The Governor General of Canada

## Origins

The Queen of Great Britain is also the Queen of Canada. The Governor General is the Monarch's representative in Canada and she or he is authorized to "exercise, on the advice of her or his Canadian Ministers, all Her Majesty's powers and authorities in respect of Canada." The Office of the Governor General constitutes one branch of our parliamentary system, the other two being the Senate and the House of Commons. Sections 9 and 10 of the *Constitution Act, 1867* provide for these.

Canada is a constitutional monarchy. Basically, that type of government means that the laws which govern Canada (the Constitution) recognize Queen Elizabeth II as Canada's Head of State.

The Canadian Constitution dates back to Confederation. In 1867, the British Parliament passed the *British North America Act*, the founding document of Canada as an independent nation. Drafted by Canadians, who became known as the Fathers of Confederation, the document stated that "The Executive Government and Authority of and over Canada is hereby declared to continue and be vested in The Queen."

In 1982, the Canadian Parliament passed the *Constitution Act, 1982*, which provided, for the first time in our country's history, a way of "amending" or changing the Constitution without having to obtain the approval of the British Parliament each time a change was required. This "patriation" or "bringing home" of the Canadian Constitution did not alter The Queen's status in Canada as Head of State. Her personal representative in Canada remains the Governor General, whose powers and authorities are detailed in the "Letters Patent Constituting the Office of the Governor General of Canada" (1 October 1947).

As in many constitutional monarchies, there is a clear separation in roles between the Head of State and the Head of Government. Canada's Head of State is the Queen (who is represented by the Governor General—The

Governor General is appointed by the Queen on the advice of the Canadian Prime Minister). Canada's Head of Government is the Prime Minister who is an elected representative.

The tradition of appointing a Canadian to the office of Governor General began in 1952, with the appointment of Vincent Massey, followed by the appointment of Georges Vanier in 1959. At the same time, a custom of alternating persons from English and French-speaking backgrounds developed. The Right Honourable Jeanne Sauvé (Governor General 1984-1990) was the first woman named to the post.

His Excellency the Right Honourable Roméo LeBlanc was appointed Governor General of Canada on 22 November 1994 and was sworn into office on 8 February 1995. He is the twenty-fifth Governor General since Confederation.

## *Role*

The Office of the Governor General includes a number of responsibilities which are constitutional and traditional in nature. These responsibilities fall under six major themes: The Crown In Canada, Canadian Sovereignty, Recognition of Excellence, National Identity, National Unity and Moral Leadership.

The Governor General fulfills a number of obligations associated with The Crown In Canada (the legal entity which embodies the Government). Representing the Queen, the Governor General or an appointed deputy gives 'Royal Assent' to bills passed by the House of Commons and the Senate, thereby establishing the bills as Acts of Parliament (the laws of Canada). The Governor General also summons, prorogues (ends a session) and dissolves Parliament (ends Parliament until a new one is sworn in after an election); delivers the Speech from the Throne at the opening of sessions (outlining the Government's plans for legislation); signs State documents (documents requiring and authorizing particular appointments and actions) such as Orders-in-Council, commissions and pardons; and presides over the swearing-in of the Prime Minister of Canada, the Chief Justice of Canada, Cabinet Ministers and other members of the Privy Council.

By constitutional convention, the Governor General has the right to be consulted, to encourage and to warn. One of the Governor General's most important responsibilities is to ensure that Canada always has a Prime Minister. Should this position become vacant through death, resignation, parliamentary stalemate or party dissension, the Governor General must provide a replacement.

In addition to the above responsibilities, the Governor General receives the Queen and other members of the Royal Family on royal visits to Canada. The Governor General is the Commander-in-Chief of the Canadian Forces. The Governor General and his wife are Canada's hosts to visiting heads of state and other distinguished visitors. They also extend their hospitality in many ways to a large number of Canadians and take part in numerous public activities. When foreign countries appoint their ambassadors or High Commissioners to Canada, the Governor General accepts their letters of credence or letters of commission.

The Governor General recognizes excellence through the Canadian Honours System. In the national context, "honours" are defined as orders, decorations and medals granted or awarded by the Governor General on behalf of The Queen. The Canadian Honours System recognizes achievement, bravery, exemplary or meritorious service over a broad range of activity.

In keeping with the ancient practice that heraldry (the study, use and regulation of coats of arms) flows from The Queen, the Governor General also heads the Canadian Heraldic Authority. Since its creation in 1988, the Authority has granted arms to corporations, governments, academic, cultural and religious institutions as well as individuals.

The Governor General attends aboriginal and ethnic events. She or he also participates in a wide range of cultural programs, and receives Canadians from every walk of life.

Travel is an essential activity, and an effective means by which to promote national unity. The Governor General goes to the provinces and the territories on a regular basis, meeting with the Lieutenant-Governors (The Queen's provincial representatives), participating in events ranging from international conferences to civic receptions, giving speeches and interviews, visiting schools and hospitals and participating in events held by the organizations of which the Governor General is Honorary Patron.

The Governor General demonstrates moral leadership through association with numerous national service organizations, youth groups and humanitarian endeavours. For example, the Governor General is Chief Scout of Canada, Honorary President of the Canadian Red Cross Society and Patron of many organizations and events.

# Governors General of Canada
## Since Confederation—1867-1995

The Viscount Monck
1867-1868

Lord Lisgar
1868-1872

The Earl of Dufferin
1872-1878

The Earl of Aberdeen
1893-1898

The  Earl of Minto
1898-1904

Earl Grey
1904-1911

The Viscount Willingdon
1926-1931

The Earl of Bessborough
1931-1935

Lord Tweedsmuir
1935-1940

Georges-P. Vanier
1959-1967

Roland Michener
1967-1974

Jules Léger
1974-1979

The Marquess of Lorne
1878-1883

The Marquess of Lansdowne
1883-1888

Lord Stanley
1888-1893

H.R.H. The Duke of Connaught
1911-1916

The Duke of Devonshire
1916-1921

Lord Byng of Vimy
1921-1926

The Earl of Athlone
1940-1946

The Viscount Alexander
1946-1952

Vincent Massey
1952-1959

Edward Schreyer
1979-1984

Jeanne Sauvé
1984-1990

Ramon John Hnatyshyn
1990-1995

Romeo Leblanc
1995-

19

*The Senate is seen in session.*

# Chapter 4

# *The Senate*

## *Origins*

The second branch of Parliament, the Senate, is the appointed body of our parliamentary system. When the Senate was established in 1867, it was intended to play two important roles:

1. to give equal representation to the various regions of Canada, and

2. to act as a regulating body that would provide a break on any hasty or ill-considered legislation initiated in the elected House.

Why these two roles?

First, the establishment of a Senate was seen as a means of protecting the less-populated of the three main areas that were to become Canada in 1867. Since representation in the House of Commons was to be based on population, the less-populated areas felt that their needs would not be looked after in a House dominated by representatives from the more heavily populated areas. The Senate, therefore, was created to represent the various regional interests in Canada in the process leading to the enactment of federal laws.

Second, in the enactment of those laws, the Senate was established not to duplicate but to complement the legislative role of the House of Commons. As Sir John A. MacDonald said, the Senate was to be a "House of sober second thought."

## *Role*

Today, the Senate still protects regional interests, but its main function is to review legislation passed by the House of Commons. No legislation passed by the House of Commons can become law until all three branches of Parliament have accepted it in the same form. When the Senate receives the proposed legislation in the form of a bill from the House of Commons, the Senate can do one of three things. Like the House of Commons, it can pass the bill without amendment; it can amend it; or it can reject the bill in its entirety. If the Senate makes an amendment to the bill, the House of Commons has the option of either accepting or rejecting it. If the House of Commons rejects the amendment, the bill is returned to the Senate and the Senate must then decide whether or not it will insist on the amendment. If the Senate insists on its amendment and the House of Commons continues to disagree, then that particular bill may be withdrawn and possibly re-introduced at a future date, or it may die on the *Order Paper* at the end of a session.

The Senate, like the House of Commons, is empowered to introduce bills, with one exception: it cannot introduce taxation bills or bills that authorize the spending of public funds. According to the *Constitution Act, 1867*, the House of Commons is the only branch of Parliament that holds such power.

The Senate also plays an important role through its committee work. Detailed consideration of legislation by its committees has been of immeasurable benefit to Canadians. From time to time, Senate committees look into social, public, and international problems or issues concerning all Canadians. Their thorough and intricate study of these issues has been of valuable assistance to Canadians and has led to innovations and changes to government policy based on committee recommendations. Canadians will remember the important studies and recommendations put forth by the Special Senate Committee on Poverty, and the Special Senate Committee on Aging. Both committee reports were used by the Canadian Government as a foundation in developing policies on these two important social problems. More recently, a Special Senate Committee completed its study of euthanasia and assisted suicide and, in its report to the Senate, consolidated a considerable amount of research and data in the area.

## Composition

When the Senate was created in 1867, it consisted of three divisions: Ontario, Quebec, and the Maritime provinces (Nova Scotia and New Brunswick). Ontario and Quebec were given twenty-four senators each and Nova Scotia and New Brunswick were given a combined total of twenty-four Senators. In 1915, a fourth division comprising the western provinces was also given a combined total of twenty-four senators. As each new province joined Confederation (Manitoba in 1870, British Columbia in 1871, Prince Edward Island in 1873, Saskatchewan and Alberta in 1905, and Newfoundland in

1949), they too were given representation in the Senate. Parliament passed an act in 1975 entitling the Yukon Territory and the Northwest Territories to be represented in the Senate by one Senator each. The 104 seats in the Senate are distributed as follows: Ontario, 24; Quebec, 24; Nova Scotia, 10; New Brunswick, 10; Manitoba, 6; British Columbia, 6; Prince Edward Island, 4; Saskatchewan, 6; Alberta, 6; Newfoundland, 6; Yukon Territory, 1; and the Northwest Territories, 1. There is also a provision in the Constitution to allow for the appointment of an additional four or eight Senators in the event of a deadlock between the two Houses. However, this provision has been used only once in Canadian history, in 1990.

## Eligibility

Senators are appointed in the Queen's name by the Governor General on the advice of the Prime Minister until they reach the age of seventy-five. Prior to 1965, all Senators were appointed for life.

To be considered for an appointment to the Senate, a candidate must:

1. be at least thirty years of age;
2. be a Canadian citizen;
3. be the owner of property worth at least $4,000.00, after debts, in the province to which the candidate is appointed;
4. have at least an additional $4,000.00 of personal property after debts and liabilities; and
5. be a resident of the province for which the candidate is appointed. In the case of Quebec, the candidate must have real property qualification in the electoral division for which she or he is appointed or be a resident of that division.

Once an individual is appointed to the Senate, certain conditions must be met to prevent removal from office. A Senator may lose her or his seat if she or he:

1. fails to attend in the Senate for two consecutive sessions of Parliament;
2. gives up Canadian citizenship;
3. becomes bankrupt or a public defaulter;
4. is attainted of treason or convicted of a felony or any infamous crime; or
5. no longer meets the property requirement.

Senators who wish to resign their seat in the Senate may do so by submitting a letter of resignation to the Governor General of Canada.

Prior to 1929, women were not eligible to be appointed to the Senate. At that time, the Judicial Committee of the Privy Council ruled that women could be considered for appointment to the Senate, and in 1930, a woman, Cairine Reay Wilson, was for the first time appointed to the Senate.

Senators are paid $64,400 per year and have a tax-free expense allowance of $10,100.[1]

---

[1] This information is based on January, 1996 figures.

# Chapter 5

# *The House of Commons*

The third branch of Parliament, the House of Commons, is unquestionably the most influential and important. It is composed of representatives elected from all parts of the country to serve the people of Canada.

## *Origins*

The House of Commons, like the Senate, was officially created in 1867 with the enactment of the Canadian Constitution. It is clear from the wording of the Constitution that the British House of Commons was intended to be the model for its Canadian counterpart. The basic provisions concerning the House of Commons are contained in sections 37 to 52 of the Constitution. These provisions reflect many of the structures and procedures of the British Commons. In addition to these sections, Section 18, states that both the Senate and House of Commons will have "powers, privileges and immunities" no greater than those held and exercised by the British House of Commons at the time of Confederation.

Thus, although the Canadian House of Commons had its formal beginning in the Constitution, its historical origins as a parliamentary institution reach back to thirteenth-century England. At that time, the knights, who represented the shires (counties), and the burgesses, who represented the boroughs (cities), were summoned by the King when he was in need of money. These representatives of the people became known as "the Commons." They met and debated separately from another already well-established group of royal officials and advisers, the barons and the bishops, who had become known as the Peers or "Lords spiritual and temporal."

## *Today*

It became a practice of the Commons, in the early days, to insist, as a condition for granting money to the King, that their grievances be settled.

*The House of Commons Chamber with the House in session.*

This practice later became a recognized right of the Commons and is today one of the underlying principles associated with the voting of supply—the money needed by the government to cover its expenditures in a given period of time. Although the Monarch's executive powers have long since been assumed by a government elected by the people, the right to discuss grievances and insist that they be resolved before granting funds is continued in the procedure for "allotted days," also known as "opposition days" or "supply days."

There are twenty such days in each fiscal year on which the Opposition can, after giving twenty-four hours' notice, initiate a debate on any matter that it chooses. (Should the House sit or not sit on days it is scheduled to, this number of opposition days may be increased or decreased proportionately.) Under this procedure, the Opposition is given an opportunity to make its views known to the House and to the public as to why supply should not be granted. On eight of these supply days, a vote may be taken on the matter raised by the Opposition.

There are, of course, other specific occasions such as each day during the time allotted for Members' Statements and for Question Period, as well as during the debate on the Throne Speech and the debate that follows the presentation of a budget, when the Opposition can express its dissatisfaction with the government. In taking advantage of these opportunities, Opposition members are, in effect, reacting to the government's requests for supply just as the knights and burgesses reacted when the King summoned them together to ask for the money he needed to govern the country.

## Functions

One of the principal functions of the House of Commons is to serve as a public forum for the free discussion of important social and political issues. In fulfilling this function, it represents popular opinion and serves both as a support of and a check on the actions of the government. For example, with respect to the House of Commons serving as a check on government, free discussion of important social and political issues can expose shortcomings of the government of the day and lead to the loss of confidence by the House of Commons. If this happens, the government will be dissolved and either a new government will be sworn in or a general election will be called. Accordingly, the desire of government to avoid this fate encourages it to maintain a degree of competence and professionalism sufficient to meet the standards of the House of Commons. Hence the check on government.

Another principal function of the House of Commons is to make laws. This role is shared with the Senate since every law must be passed by both Houses in the identical form before it can receive Royal Assent and come into effect. A detailed description of how laws are made is contained in Chapter 11.

A third principal function of the House of Commons is the control of finance. This function is carried out through the study and adoption of the Budget, Estimates, Appropriation Acts, taxation bills and other money bills, almost all of which, under the Constitution, must originate in the House of Commons.

## *Composition*

The principle underlying the composition of the House of Commons is that of representation by population, or as George Brown, one of the Fathers of Confederation, insisted, "Rep. by Pop." Thus, each province is represented in proportion to its population. At the time of Confederation, the total number of members in the House of Commons was 181, divided as follows: Ontario, 82; Quebec, 65; Nova Scotia, 19; and New Brunswick, 15. Every ten years, following the census, the number of seats for each province is adjusted in accordance with changes in the population.

Currently, there are 295 seats in the House of Commons, allocated as follows: Ontario, 99; Quebec, 75; Nova Scotia, 11; New Brunswick, 10; Manitoba, 14; British Columbia, 32; Prince Edward Island, 4; Saskatchewan, 14; Alberta, 26; Newfoundland, 7; the Yukon Territory, 1; and the Northwest Territories, 2. Elections held in 1997 or later will increase the number of seats to 301. This six-seat increase will be allocated to Ontario which increases its present seat allocation from 99 to 103 and to British Columbia which increases from 32 to 34 seats. To protect the representation of the smaller provinces, the Constitution provides that the number of Members representing a province in the House of Commons may not be less than the number of its Senators.

## *Duties of Members*

The first duty of Members of the House of Commons is to represent the interests of their constituencies. They do this by participating in the debates of the House of Commons where they can express their views on government policies, especially those policies contained in government bills. They also have an opportunity to take an active part in the various committees of the House where matters of public interest are examined.

Since the House of Commons operates on the basis of party discipline, each Member owes allegiance to the political party to which she or he belongs. Therefore, the views of that party will invariably be reflected in the Member's reaction to, and comments on, government policies and decisions, whether expressed in the House of Commons or in committee.

In addition to their duties in the House and its committees, Members also participate in the regular meetings of their party caucuses. At the same time, they try to keep in close contact with their constituencies so that they can be aware of the views of their electors on important national and local issues and can assist their constituents with any difficulties they may have in dealing with government departments.

N° 0884

INITIALES DU SCRUTATEUR

SPACE FOR INITIALS OF D.R.O.

ÉLECTION GÉNÉRALE
CIRCONSCRIPTION DE
BELLEVILLE, ONT.

GENERAL ELECTION
ELECTORAL DISTRICT OF
BELLEVILLE, ONT.

SPÉCIMEN

1975

JOUR DU SCRUTIN / POLLING DAY
Septembre 15 September 1975

Imprimé par:     Printed by:

THOMAS MARTIN
340 rue Montcalm St.,
Clarenceville, Ont.

CANADA

*Back View of Ballot Paper with
Numbered Counterfoil*

DOE, John
••• Indépendant / Independent •••

DOE, William
Appartenance politique/Political Affiliation

UNTEL, Paul

UNTEL, Pierre-Paul
Appartenance politique/Political Affiliation

*Ballot Paper presently used for General Elections*

# Chapter 6

# Electing Our Representatives

Canadians who wish to become members of the House of Commons may do so if they follow the procedures and meet the guidelines described in this chapter.

## Representation

The House of Commons bases its membership on representation by population, and the number of representatives is adjusted after each ten year census. Up until 1997, the House of Commons will have 295 Members of Parliament, commonly referred to as MPs, representing all of Canada. This number increases to 301 in 1997, as a result of the representation order of 1996.

What method is used to elect these representatives? To begin with, each Member of the House of Commons is elected by the residents of an electoral district, also known as a "riding" or "constituency." These electoral districts are revised and drawn up by independent electoral boundaries commissions. In order to ensure that every part of Canada is represented in the House of Commons, there is one commission for each of the ten provinces and for the Northwest Territories. (The Yukon Territory consists of only one electoral district and therefore requires no commission.)

## Qualification to run for elected office

Any Canadian citizen, 18 years of age or older is eligible to become a candidate for election to the House of Commons unless they have been convicted of certain offences under the *Canada Elections Act* or are incarcerated in a correctional institution. There are, however, certain Canadians who are ineligible because of the public positions they hold. These include: most judges, Senators; Members of provincial or territorial legislatures; and the Chief and Assistant Chief Electoral Officer of Canada.

31

## *Obtaining the nomination*

Long before the Prime Minister announces the date of an election, the officers of the various political party associations in each electoral district are busy organizing and holding nomination meetings to present their favourite or endorsed candidate, who will be ready to "run" at the start of the election campaign. At these nomination meetings, members of a political party gather to elect the person, who in their view, stands the best chance of winning the seat against candidates from competing parties. Prior to the nomination meeting, the candidates have an opportunity to sell memberships to residents in their electoral district with the aim of having as many people as possible attend the nomination meeting to support them. Normally, parties have cut-off dates for the sale of these memberships incorporated in their party constitution.

During the nominating meeting, the candidates who wish to win their party's endorsement have an opportunity to speak to association members in order to convince the members that they are best suited to become the official candidate. After the speeches are completed, the delegates have an opportunity to vote by secret ballot for the purpose of selecting the "chosen one" or "nominee." This official party candidate, when elected, will be eligible to "run" under that party's banner in the forthcoming election whenever it is held. It is not unusual to see these nominating meetings being held to select official candidates one or two years prior to the call of a general election. This is done in order to enable candidates to organize their campaigns and to allow them to become better known and identified with their party's platform and policies. Sometimes, candidates who cannot elicit the support or endorsement of a registered political party will run as "independent" candidates. Though any candidate may succeed, they may have a difficult time being elected since they do not have a party organization behind them. Those who have succeeded have been candidates with a proven performance record. Only a very few candidates have managed to get elected to the House of Commons as independents.

## *Name on ballot*

Once the Prime Minister calls the election, there are certain steps the candidates must follow in order to ensure that their names appear on the ballot paper. First of all, they must be officially nominated, that is, the candidate must obtain the support and signatures of 100 or more qualified electors who reside in the electoral district the candidate is seeking to represent. Second, they must appoint an official agent (their financial manager) and an auditor. Third, a $1,000.00 deposit must be paid to the Receiver General for Canada (half of this is reimbursed if their election expenses return and unused official receipts are submitted within the required time, and the balance if the candidate has obtained at least 15 percent of the valid votes cast). This deposit, along with the nomination papers containing the 100 or more signatures, must be submitted to the returning officer of the candidate's electoral district at least four weeks before election day. If the returning officer is satisfied that the candidate has properly submitted the deposit, nominating papers, and other required documents as spelled out in the *Canada Elections Act,* the returning officer will issue a "receipt of nomination" as official proof of the candidate's nomination. This will ensure that the candidate will have their name appear on the ballot paper.

## The road to victory

Candidates who are serious about being elected have a lot of work to do in order to win the support of the voters in their electoral district. Almost from the night of their nomination victory and right up to election day, the candidates and their supporters travel extensively throughout their electoral district, making speeches at various public functions. Many will also attempt to knock on every door in their riding trying to convince the voters to support them. The candidates' supporters will be working hard preparing and handing out literature on their candidate and the policies their candidate supports. The supporters will also display pictures of their candidate in public places in order to make their candidate's face, name, and slogan familiar to as many potential voters as possible. One can assume that the candidate with the best organization and the most supporters working for their campaign will have an advantage over those who cannot attract campaign supporters. It is a sign of a well-run campaign when a candidate's name becomes a household word familiar to the majority of voters in the electoral district.

## Election day

When election day finally arrives, it is usually a quiet day for the candidates, who generally spend their time resting with their families and senior aides, waiting for the results to start coming in. Under the *Canada Elections Act,* federal elections must be held on a Monday, unless that Monday falls on a statutory holiday, in which case polling day would be on the Tuesday of the same week. Voting begins at 9 a.m. and concludes at 8 p.m. (local time).

## *Term of office*

Once the candidate is elected, a trip to Ottawa must soon be made to set up an office and hire staff. This also gives the candidate an opportunity to become acquainted with the Parliament Buildings, which could be their principal base of operations for the next five years. This move to Ottawa will probably be hard on the family, as well as on the Member, for, depending on the location of the Member's electoral district, the Member may have difficulty returning home every weekend to spend time with their family. If, for example, the Member's electoral district is in British Columbia, it may mean a trip home only every two weeks because of the distance involved. In recent years, more and more Members have moved their families to Ottawa, in order to maintain a normal family life. Under our system of government, Members of the House of Commons are elected for a maximum five-year term. However, this can be shortened if the government of the day is defeated in the House of Commons or if the Prime Minister judges that an earlier election would result in the government being re-elected. Generally, if the government holds the majority of the seats in the House of Commons, the election is called in the fourth year of the five-year term.

## *Benefits as members*

Members of the House of Commons earn $64,400.00 per year,[1] plus an additional $21,300.00 to 28,200.00 per year as a tax-free expense allowance.[1] The amount of the expense allowance varies depending on the location of the electoral district. For example, a member who represents a large geographical district in the Northwest Territories, where travel to remote areas may require a chartered aircraft, would be eligible for more expense money than a member from downtown Toronto who can walk through her or his district in a few hours.

---

[1] This information is based on January 1996 figures.

## *Vacancies and by-elections*

If a vacancy occurs in the House of Commons through either resignation or death, the seat is filled by calling a by-election. Certain procedures must be followed:

1. In the case of death, two Members of the House of Commons must notify the Speaker in writing, or one can do it orally in the House of Commons, that a vacancy exists as a result of the death of their colleague. The Speaker, upon receipt of this formal notification, proceeds to address a warrant to the Chief Electoral Officer of Canada to issue a writ of election for that electoral district and announces to the House that she/he has done so.

2. In the case of a Member's resignation, the Member must tender the resignation to the Speaker of the House of Commons orally or two Members may inform the Speaker in writing. Upon receipt of this notification, the Speaker proceeds as in paragraph 1 above.

The Speaker of the House of Commons (not the Prime Minister) is the only person empowered to issue a warrant. After the Speaker announces to the House of Commons that a warrant has been issued for the particular electoral district, the Prime Minister has a maximum of six months to announce the date of the by-election. The Prime Minister can decide to hold the by-election at any time, so long as she or he has fulfilled the requirement of announcing the date within six months of the date of the issue of the warrant.

By-elections have proven to be very important to the various parties in the House of Commons because they can change the overall party standings. For example, if there were two vacancies in a 295 Member House of Commons consisting of the Liberals, governing with a minority of 130 members, the Reform Party, as the Official Opposition with 129, the Bloc Québécois with 31, the Progressive Conservatives with 1, and the independents with 2, by-election victories by the Reform Party for the 2 vacancies would significantly change the above party standings with respect to who would be able to govern and win the confidence of the House of Commons. A by-election, therefore, could change the party standings and threaten the governing minority party.

By-elections have also proven to be important to the various political parties as a test of their popularity with the voters in certain regions and as an indicator both to the government and to the opposition parties in terms of national popularity. There have been instances where governing parties have altered certain policies due to them interpreting by-election losses as displeasure by voters with the way the government was conducting the affairs of the nation. It is also important to note that should several by-elections be held consecutively, they can serve as a signal to the parties as to what the electors are thinking.

## *Chief Electoral Officer*

Canada's federal elections are administered through the Office of the Chief Electoral Officer of Canada, known as Elections Canada. Our present Chief Electoral Officer is Jean-Pierre Kingsley, who was appointed to this important position in February 1990. Mr. Kingsley is only the fifth person to hold this office since it was established by the *Dominion Elections Act* of 1920. The appointment to this position is made by a resolution of the House of Commons, and the salary attached to the position is equal to the salary of a judge of the Federal Court of Canada.

## *Who can vote?*

All Canadian citizens over 18 years of age have the right to vote in federal elections; it is such a well-established freedom that most of us take it for granted. Our democratic rights as Canadians are enshrined in the *Charter of Rights and Freedoms*. Certain Canadians, however, because of their positions or circumstances, cannot vote. These are:

1. the Chief and Assistant Chief Electoral Officers of Canada;
2. the returning officer in each electoral district (should there be a tie, the returning officer in that electoral district is empowered to cast a vote after a recount has taken place); and
3. any person who has been disqualified from voting because of corrupt or illegal practices in the past seven or five years respectively.

After each federal election, the Chief Electoral Officer, who is accountable only to Parliament, submits a report to Parliament on the election and recommends changes that, in his opinion, will improve the administration of the next election.

## Key Dates in Electoral History

### 1854

Nova Scotia adopts manhood suffrage—the first British colony in North America to grant the vote to all British male subjects who meet residence qualifications, without regard to religion or property ownership, although Native persons and paupers receiving government or county aid are specifically excluded. Manhood suffrage is abolished in 1863 and replaced by a new assessment franchise.

### 1855

New Brunswick introduces ballot voting; previously electors had to publicly declare their names and for whom they voted.

### 1867

The Confederation of Canada is created. The *British North America* Act stipulates that the provincial franchise will be used for federal elections until Parliament decides otherwise.

### 1874

The first *Dominion Elections Act* is passed, introducing the secret ballot across Canada. Electors who are illiterate or have physical disabilities may ask the deputy returning officer for assistance in marking their ballots.

### 1885

A Dominion franchise based on property ownership is instituted. In 1896, however, the franchise reverts to the provinces.

### 1915

Postal voting is introduced to enable military personnel overseas to cast their ballots. (Named the Special Voting Rules in 1970, this procedure is now available to all qualified electors who are unable to vote in person at the regular or advance polls.) For the first time, employees must have at least one hour free in addition to their lunch hour on polling day to vote.

## *1917*

All members of the armed forces, including those under 21, Native servicemen, and nurses on active military service acquire the right to vote. The franchise is also extended, without regard to property qualifications, to men with a son or grandson and women with a husband, son or brother in the armed forces.

## *1918*

Women gain the right to vote in federal elections. In 1919 they become eligible to run for seats in the House of Commons. In 1921, the first woman, Agnes MacPhail, is elected to the House of Commons.

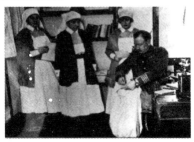

## *1920*

*The Dominion Elections Act* is completely revamped, establishing the first federal framework for the franchise and the preparation of voters lists all across Canada. Advance polling is introduced. Oliver Mowat Biggar is appointed Canada's first Chief Electoral Officer and is mandated to direct the election machinery.

## *1930*

A federal door-to-door enumeration process is established to eliminate reliance on provincial voters lists.

## *1934*

Parliament decides to draw up a permanent list of Canadian electors. The list is used in the general election of 1935 but the technology of the day is insufficient to overcome the logistical obstacles and it is abandoned in 1938.

## *1944*

Proxy voting is introduced so that Canadian prisoners of war may vote through a relative. Proxy voting is extended in 1970 and 1977 to fishermen, salesmen, trappers, airplane crews and others who cannot vote in person; in 1993 the extension of special ballot voting makes proxy voting unnecessary.

## *1948*

The last vestige of property qualification is eliminated from the franchise and candilates must now be qualified electors.

## *1960*

Native men living on reserves are enfranchised; native women on reserves must wait until 1986 before their right to vote of is finally recognized.

## *1964*

The *Electoral Boundaries Readjustment Act* is adopted, and independent commissions begin to redraw riding boundaries after each decennial census.

## *1970*

The new *Canada Elections* Act drops the voting age from 21 to 18. Political parties must register in order to field candidates at an election; in the next federal election in 1972, the political affiliation of candidates begins to appear on the ballot. (The number of registered parties increased from four to fourteen between 1972 to 1993.)

## *1974*

Legislation is passed to limit the election expenses of parties and candidates and to provide for reimbursement from the public treasury. A Commissioner is appointed to enforce the new legislation and, in 1977, the Commissioner's mandate is extended to all aspects of the *Canada Elections Act.*

## *1982*

*The Canadian Charter of Rights and Freedoms* entrenches in the Constitution the right of all citizens to vote and to be a candidate.

## *1992*

*The Referendum Act* is the first federal legislation permitting referendums on constitutional matters. For the first time, at the 1992 federal referendum, the lists of electors are computerized on CD-ROM.

*The Canada Elections Act* is amended by Bill C-78 to ensure that the electoral process is accessible to persons with disabilities. The Act now provides for mobile polling stations, templates for the use of voters who are blind or visually impaired, transfer certificates for voters with disabilities and level access at all polling stations. The Chief Electoral Officer has a mandate to implement public education and information programs to make the electoral process better known to the public, especially to those most likely to experience difficulties in exercising democratic rights.

## *1993*

Bill C-114 amends the *Canada Elections Act* to ensure that all Canadians eligible to vote have a means of exercising their franchise. Special ballot voting is extended to Canadians living or travelling outside the country and inmates serving sentences of less than two years, as well as other Canadians who cannot vote in person for any reason. Federal judges may now vote, as may persons with mental disabilities. The process of registering becomes more accessible to voters through mail-in registration cards and polling day registration.

# Chapter 7

## The Prime Minister,
## The Cabinet and Formation of a Government,
## The Privy Council

### The Prime Minister

*Powers*

Canadians searching for descriptions of the roles and powers of the Prime Minister would have difficulty finding this information in our Constitution because they are not mentioned. Power is not explicitly vested in the Prime Minister by law; it is exercised formally in accordance with the custom of the Constitution. Prime Ministerial power, therefore, is exercised through Constitutional convention. Among the important powers the Prime Minister alone can exercise are to make recommendations to the Governor General with regards to:

1. the appointment of Cabinet Ministers;

2. the appointment of Senators;

3. the appointment of the Chief Justice of Canada;

4. the appointment of the Lieutenant-Governors of the provinces; and

5. the timing for a dissolution and for a summoning of Parliament.

*Eligibility*

The Prime Minister is invariably a Member of the House of Commons, although there have been two occasions, in 1891-1892 and in 1894-1896, when the Prime Minister was a Senator. Should an individual who is not a Member of the House of Commons become Prime Minister, the person would, by convention, usually seek election as soon as possible.

## Canada's Prime Ministers Since Confederation

*Sir John A. MacDonald,*
*1867-1873, 1878-1891*

*A. Mackenzie,*
*1873-1878*

*Sir J.I. Abbott,*
*1891-1892*

*Sir John Thompson,*
*1892-1894*

*Sir Mackenzie Bowell,*
*1894-1896*

*Sir Charles Tupper,*
*1896*

*Sir Wilfrid Laurier,*
*1896-1911*

*Sir Robert L. Borden,*
*1911-1920*

*Arthur Meighen,*
*1920-1921, 1926*

*W.L. Mackenzie King,*
*1921-1930, 1933-1948*

*R.B. Bennett,*
*1930-1935*

*Louis S. St. Laurent,*
*1948-1957*

*John G. Diefenbaker,*
*1957-1963*

*Lester B.Pearson,*
*1963-1968*

*Joseph Clark,*
*1979-1980*

*Pierre E. Trudeau,*
*1968-1979, 1980-1984*

*John N. Turner*
*June to September 1984*

*Brian M. Mulroney*
*Septembre 1984-1988,*
*1988-June 1993*

*Kim Campbell*
*June to November 1993*

*Jean Chrétien*
*November 1993-*

Canada has had twenty different individuals serve as Prime Minister since Confederation. The leader of the party winning the largest number of seats in the House of Commons following an election will usually be called on by the Governor General to form a government. The Prime Minister and the government depend on the support of a majority of the Members of the House of Commons. Generally, a Prime Minister who loses the support of the majority of the Members in the House of Commons on an important initiative would have little choice but to resign or to appeal to the voters in a general election. In addition to this, the Constitution requires that a House of Commons, if not dissolved sooner, expires after five years, thus governments are obliged periodically to seek a new mandate from the electorate.

As stated in Chapter 3, one of the most important duties of the Governor General is to ensure Canada always has a Prime Minister. If a government loses the confidence of the House, the Governor General could ask the Leader of the Opposition to form a new government as an alternative to dissolving the Parliament. In such a case, the Governor General would probably need to be assured that the Leader of the Opposition had the confidence of the House of Commons and could govern without being defeated.

## Renumeration

The Prime Minister receives an annual salary of $69,920.00 in addition to the salary received as a member of Parliament.[1]

## The Prime Minister's Office

The Prime Minister's Office is organized into a secretariat and has the staff to keep the Prime Minister aware of all significant developments throughout the country. It also:

1. assists the Prime Minister with parliamentary duties;
2. arranges public appearances that are usually associated with government business;
3. prepares letters and messages that the Prime Minister must send in reply to correspondence and requests; and

---

[1] This information is based on January, 1996 figures.

4.  arranges appointments for individuals and delegations that have briefs to submit to the government.

# The Cabinet and
# Formation of a Government

As in the case of the Prime Minister, the Constitution makes no specific mention of the Cabinet, despite the fact that it is the supreme policy-making body in our system of government.

## *Cabinet Eligibility and Selection*

The Cabinet is composed of Ministers headed by the Prime Minister and is technically a committee of the Privy Council. A person appointed to a prestigious Cabinet position must take an Oath as a Privy Councillor and an Oath of Office for the ministerial duty they will assume.

The majority of members of a Cabinet are chosen from the House of Commons. In addition to the House of Commons, the Senate is usually represented by a least one member, namely, the Leader of the Government in the Senate. A minister appointed from outside Parliament is generally expected to gain election to the House of Commons at the earliest opportunity.

Although the norm for most of the 1980s was to have a Cabinet consisting of close to 40 members, there are usually about 30 members in a Cabinet. Prime Minister Chrétien's Cabinet, appointed just after the 1993 election, comprised 24 ministers, including the Prime Minister, and nine Secretaries of State.

The selection of a Cabinet is the sole responsibility of the Prime Minister and she or he alone is responsible for recommending to the Governor General who should be appointed to the Cabinet. In making her or his recommendations, the Prime Minister will take into account certain considerations. Where possible, the Prime Minister will attempt to select at least one member from each province in order to ensure the widest geographical representation. This sometimes proves to be difficult if the government of the day lacks representation in certain parts of the country. Ethnic, racial, gender and religious considerations also play a part in determining the composition of the cabinet. The Prime Minister will also appoint persons with the skills, knowledge, or other special endowments that give them a claim to be included in the government.

## *Role and Responsibility*

Three of the most important roles cabinet members perform are:

1. proposing laws by initiating government bills;
2. taking responsibility for government departments; and
3. making certain appointments, such as Judges (who are nominated by the Minister of Justice).

The Cabinet is the policy-forming body of the government and is bound by collective responsibility. Most Cabinet members are assigned government departments for which they are directly responsible. Some have non-departmental assignments (i.e. a Minister without portfolio). With the formation of the Cabinet in 1993, Prime Minister Chrétien also instituted a new type of position called a Secretary of State. Those holding the positions of Secretaries of State do not hold responsibility for any particular department, but rather are responsible for certain subject areas or agencies which may in fact cross the responsibilities of several government departments.

As the Opposition members in the House of Commons have an opportunity daily in the Question Period to question the ministers about the policies and administration of their departments, it becomes vital to Cabinet Ministers to be well informed about the departments they are in charge of. They are, therefore, regularly briefed by their senior staff.

The minister can answer for her or his stewardship in terms of the actions and performance of the branch of government for which she or he is responsible. It is important to note that the daily work of administration is carried on by public servants. The deputy ministers, or permanent heads of the departments, are expected to implement the policies determined by the Cabinet.

One of the most important functions of the Cabinet is to bring legislation into Parliament. The majority of government legislation is introduced in the House of Commons. The policy content of each bill is formulated by the Cabinet and the department concerned. Collectively, the Cabinet determines and initiates all government policy; but the check on its actions is that, in all matters, it is accountable and responsible to the House of Commons. This is the principle of responsible government.

## *Meetings and Solidarity*

The Cabinet usually meets once a week in a special room. Meetings are held in complete secrecy. No one other than the members of the Cabinet, the Clerk of the Privy Council and certain senior public servants are allowed to attend, and all discussions remain secret. In fact, all Cabinet members are sworn to secrecy upon joining the Cabinet.

When the meetings are convened, the Prime Minister, who sits at the head of the table, acts as the chairperson. Given that Cabinet solidarity is of the utmost importance to a government, Cabinet decisions are binding on all ministers and if a Cabinet member cannot support a decision, she or he will normally resign.

## *Recognition and Renumeration*

Cabinet members are entitled to the prefix "Honourable" for life by virtue of their membership in the Privy Council. They are also financially compensated with a salary of $46,645.00 per year in addition to their salaries as Members of Parliament.[1]

## The Privy Council

Section 11 of the *Constitution Act, 1867*, states that "There shall be a council to aid and advise in the Government of Canada, to be styled the Queen's Privy Council for Canada." Accordingly, the first members of the Queen's Privy Council for Canada were sworn in at Ottawa by Governor General Viscount Monck on July 1, 1867. The Council is an advisory body to the Crown, although in practice only the cabinet fulfills this role. Membership is determined by the Governor General on the advice of the Prime Minister and members are appointed for life. Cabinet members of a government in power constitute a committee of the Privy Council.

It is not necessary to be a member of Cabinet to be appointed to the Privy Council. When Canada celebrates special historic moments, the Governor General on the advice of the Prime Minister may appoint provincial premiers,

---

[1] This information is based on January, 1996 figures.

federal party leaders, and others to the Privy Council. For example, during our centennial in 1967, the Prime Minister of the day, Lester B. Pearson, admitted all provincial premiers to this distinguished body.

In 1982, when the Queen was in Canada to sign the proclamation that brought into effect the patriation of our Constitution, the provincial premiers and Mr. Ed Broadbent, the then Leader of the New Democratic Party (NDP) in the House of Commons, were all appointed Privy Councillors. Also, in 1984, the Prime Minister of the day, Mr. Trudeau, nominated the Leader of Her Majesty's Official Opposition, Mr. Mulroney (a future Prime Minister), as a member. At that time, Mr. Trudeau expressed his view that future Leaders of the Opposition, if not already members of the Privy Council, should, by virtue of office, be sworn in as Privy Councillors. In 1991, the Prime Minister of the day, Brian Mulroney, appointed the NDP Leader, Audrey McLaughlin, to the Privy Council so that she might attend privileged briefings on the Gulf War.

*Confederation Hall, the Main Entrance to the Centre Block.*

# Chapter 8

## Opposition Parties in the House of Commons, The House Leaders, The Party Whips

### The Official Opposition

*History*

Because we inherited our present system of government from Great Britain, we expect to see similarities. Canada, like Great Britain, has a party system. As in Great Britain, Canada's opposition parties sit on the benches opposite from the government. Opposition parties are a very important part of our system of government. The opposition party that elects the second highest number of representatives to the House usually becomes the "Official Opposition," and is referred to as "Her Majesty's Loyal Opposition." Any other party that manages to elect at least twelve members to the House of Commons is also recognized as an opposition party, its leader will receive a party leader's salary and the party will be provided with research funds.

*Composition*

In the 1993 election, representatives from the Liberal Party, the Bloc Québécois, the Reform Party, the New Democratic Party and the Progressive Conservative Party were elected to the House of Commons. One independent member was also elected.

*Role*

Canada's opposition parties have several roles to play in order to be effective:

1. they should examine all proposals and policies of the governing party;

2. they should try to persuade the governing party to accept suggestions to improve its legislation; and

3. they should always be willing and able to replace the governing party by offering sound alternative solutions and policies.

While it is usually true that the cabinet controls the legislation presented in the House of Commons, the opposition should always put forward constructive criticism of the government, because the Leader of the Official Opposition is often viewed as an alternative Prime Minister. The opposition leaders should always be prepared to take over the reins of government if they manage to defeat the government in the House of Commons (on votes of confidence), or in a general election.

The opposition members of the House of Commons are responsible for questioning and criticizing the government's policies and actions. They may suggest alternative proposals to those of the government, and sometimes, if the government finds that these proposals are sound and constructive, it may decide to incorporate them into its legislation. Because the electorate views the opposition parties as alternatives to the party in power, they should always be ready with formulated policies and programs.

## *The Battleground*

Question Period, which takes place daily in the House of Commons, is one of the main battlegrounds between the government and the opposition parties. It is designed to expose weaknesses on the part of the government or on the part of the opposition parties in the exchange of questions and answers between opposition members and the Prime Minister and her or his ministers. If the opposition parties are to impress the electorate, then the Question Period is the ideal opportunity to "show up" the government and to score political points.

Caution is required, though, for the opposition parties must attempt to avoid making embarrassing mistakes in their facts when attacking government policies. If the opposition parties do not have their facts straight, and the government demonstrates this, it could prove embarrassing. It is important for opposition parties to be careful not to attack or stall government measures just for the sake of doing so. This might be seen by the electorate and the media as obstructive and may hurt an opposition party's credibility.

## *Televising the Debates*

The House of Commons began televising its debates in 1977, and since that time it has been noted that the debates have been livelier and more animated. The opposition parties, aware that thousands of viewers are watching them, do their utmost to dig deep into the heart of Cabinet policies, trying to flush out anything that may discredit the government.

## *Renumeration*

As mentioned earlier, twelve or more members must be elected to the House of Commons from a particular party for that party to be recognized as a party in the House of Commons, and to become eligible for public funds for research bureaus. The Leader of the Official Opposition is paid $49,100.00 annually for holding this position, and the leaders of the other recognized parties who have twelve or more members are paid $29,500.00 per year. This money is in addition to the salaries received as Members of the House of Commons.[1]

# The House Leaders

Government-sponsored legislation is initiated by the cabinet and the task of ensuring its passage within a reasonable time frame in the House of Commons is the responsibility of a Cabinet member called the Government House Leader. Each opposition party in the House of Commons also usually has a Member whom its appoints as its party House Leader.

## *Role and function*

Since all bills are required to follow a series of stages (introduction and first reading, second reading, committee stage, report stage, and third reading) before they can become law, certain government-sponsored bills may have priority over others because of their urgency. The Government House Leader receives instructions from the Prime Minister and Cabinet as to which bills

---

[1] This information is based on January, 1996 figures.

should be dealt with on a priority basis.

In attempting to fulfill the government's wishes, the Government House Leader will meet with her or his counterparts from the opposition parties to negotiate the order of business. She or he does this in the hope of avoiding procedural delaying tactics that may be used by opposition parties to slow the progress of government business. These meetings may also serve to satisfy an opposition party's priorities. Accordingly, every attempt is made to reach agreement through compromise. If compromise is not possible, the government has certain measures available to it. For example, the government may opt to use closure (usually used for motions) or time allocation (used for bills) to limit debate on an item. The Standing Orders of the House provide the government with options to limit debate on bills either with, or without, the agreement of opposition parties. While the government usually prefers to negotiate agreements with other parties, it may have to allocate time on legislation without the agreement of the other parties, especially when dealing with bills to which the opposition is opposed.

## The Party Whips

Every party in the House of Commons appoints a member to act as its whip. The person who acts as whip ensures that the party's members can be located when a vote is called in the House of Commons.

Members who are required to be away from the House of Commons and the parliamentary precinct to attend to other business, such as meeting with constituents or special interest groups, usually notify the whip of their location, so they can be reached to return to the House of Commons Chamber if a vote is called. Votes during which Members names are recorded are known as recorded divisions. Should the government lose a vote in the House, it could conceivably be defeated. This is why it is imperative for Members to notify their party whip of their whereabouts.

When a recorded vote takes place in the House of Commons, bells will ring to summon Members to come to the Chamber for the vote. Currently, the bells ring in the five buildings which house the offices of the Members of the House of Commons. These are: the Centre Block, the West Block, the East Block, the Wellington Building, and the Confederation Building. The bells also ring daily to summon Members to the House of Commons at the beginning of a sitting.

Once a vote is called, the party whips and their assistants immediately go into action by telephoning the Members wherever they may be, telling them to return to the Chamber as quickly as possible. If the vote is a recorded one, it means that the names of all those Members who were present at the time of voting will be entered and printed in the Journals and the daily "Hansard."

The party whips also play an important role in maintaining party discipline and the morale of their members.

And finally, they perform another important function by sitting on the "striking committee," a sub-committee of the Standing Committee on Procedure and House Affairs, which recommends to the House which Members of the House of Commons should be appointed to sit on the various standing, joint, legislative and special committees of the House of Commons.

## *Renumeration*

The government and official opposition whips are paid $13,200.00 per year for their duties and the whips of the other opposition parties receive $7,500.00 per year. This is in addition to the salaries they receive as Members of the House of Commons.[1]

---

[1] This information is based on January, 1996 figures.

*The Hon. Gilbert Parent, Speaker of the House of Commons, in the Speaker's Chair.*

# Chapter 9

# The Speakers of the Senate and the House of Commons, Other Presiding Officers, and Senior Officials of Parliament

## The Speaker

The Senate and the House of Commons each have a presiding officer referred to as the Speaker. These positions are provided for in the *Constitution Act, 1867*.[1]

## *Method of selection*

The Speaker of the Senate is chosen from among the Senators and is appointed by the Governor General on the advice of the Prime Minister, usually for the duration of a Parliament. In the House of Commons, the Speaker is elected by the House of Commons as soon as Parliament meets after an election, and holds office for the duration of a Parliament. She or he must be a Member of the House of Commons and represent an electoral district like any other Member.

In June 1985, the House of Commons adopted a Standing Order for the election of a Speaker by secret ballot. The first opportunity for Members of the House of Commons to elect a Speaker by "secret ballot" came in September 1986, when Speaker John Bosley tendered his resignation. On September 30, 1986, Members of the House of Commons made history by electing the Honourable John Fraser, after eleven ballots, as the first elected Speaker of the House. He was then re-elected in 1988. At the beginning of the 35th Parliament in January 1994, the Hon. Gilbert Parent was elected Speaker.

---

[1] Sections 34 and 44 of the *Constitution Act, 1867.*

*The daily Speaker's Parade entering the House of Commons Chamber.*

# *Role*

Among the most important roles of the Speaker are to maintain order and interpret the rules and practices of the House. In the Senate, the written rules are referred to as the "Rules of the Senate of Canada" and in the House of Commons they are the "Standing Orders." In addition, there is an extensive body of accumulated precedents and practices. The "Standing Orders" of the House of Commons require the neutrality of the Speaker; the Speaker does not participate in debate. The rules also state that the Speaker does not vote on any matter before the House, except to break a tie. There are no such written restrictions on the Speaker in the Senate, but over the years its Speakers, in the interests of neutrality, have increasingly adopted the practice of not participating in debates or votes.

In the House of Commons, the Speaker acts as the official spokesperson for that body and is also responsible for the internal management of the House and the operations of its branches and services.

# *Symbol of authority*

The Speaker's authority in both Houses is symbolised by a Mace, a club-like instrument which is laid on the Clerks' Table when each House sits. The Mace also accompanies the Speaker during the daily Speaker's Parade, which takes place before each sitting of the House. Visitors to Parliament may witness this ceremony, which involves the Speaker and other officers of Parliament in a parade through the halls of Parliament to the Chamber to officially open the day's sitting.

# The Deputy Speaker and Chairperson of Committees of the Whole House

The Deputy Speaker of the House of Commons, like the Speaker, is also elected to this position for the duration of a Parliament. This election, however, is not conducted by secret ballot; rather, it usually involves the nomination of a person for the position, with the House agreeing to the nomination. This officer serves a dual role as Deputy Speaker: she or he replaces the Speaker during the Speaker's absence, and acts as Chairperson of the Committee of the Whole, which involves presiding over the proceedings when the

House sits as a committee. Many taxation bills and all bills authorizing expenditures (referred to as appropriation bills) are usually considered in Committee of the Whole after second reading. The Deputy Speaker, of course, must be a Member of the House of Commons and, by the Standing Orders, must possess full and practical knowledge of the official language which is not that of the Speaker.

## The Deputy Chairperson of Committees of the Whole and the Assistant Deputy Chairperson of Committees of the Whole

The Deputy Chairperson and the Assistant Deputy Chairperson of Committees of the Whole are chosen at the beginning of each session of Parliament and are Members of the House of Commons. They share with the Deputy Speaker the duties of taking the Chair during the Speaker's absence and presiding over Committees of the Whole.

## Senior Officials of Parliament

## The Senate

### *The Clerk of the Senate and Clerk of Parliaments*

The Clerk of the Senate is appointed by Order-in-Council and has the rank of deputy minister. Under the *Publication of Statutes Act*, the person holding this position is also the Clerk of Parliaments and, as such, has custody of original Acts of Parliament assented to by the Governor General. The Clerk is also the officer commissioned to certify the authenticity of such Acts by affixing a seal of the Clerk's office.

The Clerk is responsible for recording the proceedings of the Senate, and for advising the Speaker and Senators on matters of parliamentary procedure. She or he also reads the commission appointing a new Speaker in the Chamber and administers the oath prescribed by law to new Senators. The Clerk of the Senate is also the Chief Administrative Officer of the Senate and accounts for her or his administration to the Standing Senate Committee on Internal Economy, Budgets and Administration.

### *The Law Clerk and Parliamentary Counsel*

The Law Clerk is appointed by a resolution of the Senate. As parliamentary Counsel to the Senate, the Law Clerk is responsible for giving legal advice to the Senate, to committees of the Senate and to individual Senators on constitutional questions, on matters of law and procedure affecting Parliament, and on other aspects of law, including questions relating to conflict of interest.

As legislative counsel, the Law Clerk advises Senators on the form and substance of government bills and proposed amendments thereto. On request, she or he also prepares private bills, private Members' public bills, notices of motion, notices of inquiry, amendments to bills and amendments to the Senate's rules of procedure. As corporate counsel, the Law Clerk provides advice on questions of law relating to the administration of the Senate, including contracts, labour relations and other personnel matters. The Assistant Law Clerk and Parliamentary Counsel provides assistance in performing all of these functions.

### *The Clerk Assistant*

The Clerk Assistant is appointed by resolution of the Senate and the duties of this officer include reading petitions, committee reports, orders of the day and other documents in the Chamber. This officer also takes the minutes of the proceedings in Committee of the Whole and acts as Clerk of that Committee. The Clerk Assistant assists the Clerk in the business of the Senate and carries out any such duties as may be instructed by the Clerk. She or he also advises the Speaker on the business of each sitting day and prepares all the required information and forms for the sitting. Along with the Clerk, the Clerk Assistant acts as an adviser on procedural matters.

### *Gentleman Usher of the Black Rod*

This office originated in England like all parliamentary offices, and can be traced back to the middle of the 14th century. Its name is taken from the ebony rod topped with a lion in gold which is the emblem of office. The Black Rod is responsible for supervising the administrative details pertaining to the opening of Parliament. In accordance with ancient custom, he is sent to the House of Commons to seek the attendance of that House in the Senate Chamber at the opening or prorogation of Parliament and for the Royal Assent ceremony.

Appointed by Governor-in-Council, he is responsible for the security services and certain maintenance services. Other duties include carrying out orders for the arrest of persons charged with breach of privilege or contempt of Parliament and performing special duties during conferences, special visits by dignitaries to the Senate, and the installation of a new Governor General.

# The House of Commons

### The Clerk of the House of Commons

The Clerk is the chief advisor to the Speaker and to Members of the House on many procedural and administrative subjects. Holding the rank of Deputy Minister, the Clerk is a commissioner appointed to administer the Oath of Allegiance to Members of the House. The Clerk is responsible for the safe-keeping of all papers and records of the House and has the direction and control of all its officers and clerks, subject to such orders as she or he may, from time-to-time, receive from the Speaker or from the House. The Clerk is the recording officer of the House and her or his minutes are a summary of the daily proceedings of the House. The Clerk records all divisions when votes are taken in the House. The Clerk is consulted by the Speaker and Members of the House whenever questions arise with respect to the privileges, rules, usages, and proceedings of Parliament.

### The Sergeant-at-Arms

The Sergeant-at-Arms is responsible for Parliamentary Precinct Services, which include the security services of the House of Commons and a number of other services related to the maintenance and operation of the parliamentary precinct. On all required occasions, the Sergeant-at-Arms attends the Speaker with the Mace, the symbol of the authority of the House. The Sergeant-at-Arms has a chair on the floor of the House. When required, this officer causes the removal of persons directed by the Speaker to withdraw, and takes into custody those strangers who are irregularly admitted to the House and those who are guilty of misconduct. She or he also introduces and admits the Gentleman Usher of the Black Rod from the Senate.

### The Deputy Clerk (Administrative Services)

The Deputy Clerk reports to the Speaker through the Clerk and is responsible for the following areas: parliamentary publications, broadcasting, electronic recording, computer and office automation services, financial management and control, internal audit, personnel administration, and administrative support functions (such as language training, health services, food services, purchasing and material management).

## *The Clerk Assistant (Procedural Services)*

The Clerk Assistant is one of the chief procedural advisors of the House and has responsibility for the Committees and Parliamentary Associations Directorate and the House Proceedings and Parliamentary Exchanges Directorate.

The Clerk, the Deputy Clerk, the Clerk Assistant and other Table Officers maintain the records of proceedings of the House, provide procedural advice to the occupants of the Chair and to Members of the House of Commons. They also ensure the smooth functioning of the House as it conducts its business.

## *General Legislative Counsel*

The General Legislative Counsel is appointed by the Board of Internal Economy. The Counsel and her or his staff assist private Members of the House of Commons in the drafting of bills, amendments and resolutions. When amendments are adopted to bills in the House, it is her or his office which ensures that reprints of the amended bills are produced. The office is also responsible for certifying all bills for printing and preparing parchments of bills for transmission to the Senate.

## *General Legal Counsel*

The General Legislative Counsel and members of her or his staff prepare memoranda and opinions on legal and constitutional matters and act as legal counsel to the House of Commons.

## *Speakers of the House of Commons since Confederation*

*James Cockburn,*
*1867-1874*

*T.W. Anglin,*
*1874-1879*

*J.G. Blanchet,*
*1879-1882*

*Sir G. Kirkpatrick,*
*1883-1887*

*J.A. Ouimet,*
*1887-1891*

*Peter White,*
*1891-1895*

*Sir J.D. Edgar,*
*1896-1899*

*Thomas Bain,*
*1899-1900*

*L.P. Brodeur,*
*1901-1904*

*N.A. Belcourt,*
*1904*

*R.F. Sutherland,*
*1905-1908*

*Chas. Marcil,*
*1909-1911*

*T.S. Sproule,*
*1911-1915*

*A. Sévigny,*
*1916-1917*

*E.N. Rhodes,*
*1917-1921*

*R. Lemieux,*
*1922-1930*

*George Black,*
*1930-1935*

*J.L. Bowman,*
*1935*

*P.F. Casgrain,*
*1936-1940*

*J. Allison Glen,*
*1940-1945*

*Gaspard Fauteux,*
*1945-1949*

*W. Ross MacDonald,*
*1949-1953*

*L. René Beaudoin,*
*1953-1957*

*Roland Michener,*
*1957-1962*

*Marcel Lambert,*
*1962-1963*

*Alan A. MacNaughton,*
*1963-1966*

*Lucien Lamoureux,*
*1966-1974*

*James Jerome,*
*1974-1980*

*Jeanne Sauvé,*
*1980-1984*

*Lloyd Francis,*
*January to September 1984*

*John Bosley,*
*September 1984-1986*

*John Fraser,*
*October 1986-January 1994*

*Gilbert Parent*
*January 1994-*

*The Sergeant-at-Arms places the Mace on the*
*Table of the House.*

# Chapter 10

## Opening of Parliament and
## Daily Proceedings in the House of Commons

### Opening of Parliament

The opening of Parliament takes place after each general election and a similar ceremony takes place at the beginning of each new session. Both are accompanied by an historic and impressive ceremony. The Governor General, as part of her or his duties, opens each new Parliament and each session of a Parliament. From Confederation in 1867 up until 1996, Canada has had thirty-five general elections and thus thirty-five Parliaments. Should the Queen be visiting Canada at the time of the opening of a new Parliament, she would undoubtedly be asked to open Parliament personally.

### *The Speech from the Throne*

This ceremony begins with the arrival of the Governor General on Parliament Hill by open landau (weather permitting). There she or he inspects a Guard of Honour before entering the Senate Chamber. Preceded by the Gentleman Usher of the Black Rod, the Governor General takes her or his seat on the Throne in the Senate Chamber. The Governor General then awaits the arrival of the Members of the House of Commons to the Senate Chamber. The Gentleman Usher of the Black Rod proceeds to the House of Commons Chamber to acquaint Members of that House that their attendance is required in the Senate Chamber for the purpose of hearing the Governor General read the Speech from the Throne. At the beginning of a new Parliament, Members of the House will be informed that the Governor General does not see it fit to read the Speech from the Throne until the House of Commons has elected a Speaker. Members then return to the House of Commons to elect a Speaker. Once the Speaker is elected, the Members will again be summoned to the Senate Chamber. Receiving the summons, the Members will again proceed to the Senate Chamber, this time led by the Speaker.

*The Mounties on parade for the opening of Parliament.*

Once the Members arrive, they are not permitted to enter the Senate Chamber but must stand at the Bar at the entrance to the Chamber. The Prime Minister is the only person from the House of Commons permitted to sit in the Senate Chamber, where a place is reserved for her or him next to the Governor General. Senators, Supreme Court judges and the diplomatic corps are also usually all in attendance at an opening of Parliament.

Following the claim to privileges by the Speaker of the House of Commons, the Governor General reads a Speech outlining the intentions and legislative program of the government for that session. After the Governor General finishes reading the speech, the members of the House of Commons return to their Chamber.

## Daily Proceedings in House of Commons

### *Changing the rules*

A few years ago, the House of Commons accepted recommendations for procedural reform recommended by a special committee of the House. With the aim of improving the rules and practices that govern the Canadian House of Commons, this committee considered various proposals for change submitted by parliamentarians and interested Canadians, and also studied and visited other legislatures in Canada, the United States, and Great Britain. (In Chapter 11 the importance of the "Standing Orders" as a tool to be used to ensure the orderly and organized transaction of business in the House of Commons will be discussed.)

The parliamentary lifestyle has been radically changed since the House of Commons accepted these recommendations. Canadians who attended evening sittings of the House of Commons in the past are no longer able to do so. As a result of these changes, the House sits in the evening only in special circumstances. Another important change was the introduction of a fixed parliamentary calendar. More recent changes to the calendar divided a parliamentary year into several fixed periods of approximately four weeks of sittings followed by a one-week adjournment. During the summer, at Christmas and on a few other occasions during the year, the House adjourns for periods of longer than one week. These adjournment periods allow Members to spend more time in their constituencies and the fixed calendar allows the Members of the House of Commons, by knowing when the House will adjourn and resume, to better plan their activities.

## When House meets

The House of Commons meets Monday to Friday and follows a daily routine in its proceedings to enable it to function in an orderly and organized manner. On Monday the House meets from 11:00 a.m. to 7:00 p.m.; on Tuesday and Thursday it sits from 10:00 a.m. to 7:00 p.m.; on Wednesday from 2:00 p.m. to 7:00 p.m. (Members meet in caucus on Wednesday mornings) and on Fridays from 10:00 a.m. to 2:30 p.m.. The Adjournment Debate, explained later in this chapter, takes place between 6:30 p.m. and 7:00 p.m. Monday through Thursday.

## Daily Routine Business

As mentioned earlier, the House of Commons deals with a daily routine of business agreed to by its Members and incorporated in the "Standing Orders." This routine business allows and ensures that the business of legislating—one of the prime duties of the House of Commons—is carried out in an organized and systematic manner.

The Speaker, who presides over the proceedings of the House of Commons, calls out the various orders of the day that are to be dealt with during a sitting day. Before any business is dealt with, however, the Speaker opens each day's sitting by reading Prayers.

Several items make up the routine proceedings, including the introduction of bills, the tabling of documents (submitting a document to the House so that it may be placed in the public domain), the moving of certain motions, the presentation of committee reports, the presentation of petitions, statements by ministers, etc.

Just before Question Period each day, there is a 15-minute period allotted for Statements by Members. During this period, a Member may be recognized by the Speaker to make a statement lasting not more than one minute on any subject of international, national, or local interest.

The House also provides for a daily Oral Question Period, which some people consider the highlight of a sitting day. This period, which is often unpredictable and boisterous, provides Members with an opportunity to question the Prime Minister and Cabinet Ministers on their actions and policies. Members who manage to be recognized by the Speaker for the purpose of asking a question, attempt at this time to take the Prime Minister and Cabinet to task when the galleries are full and the media is present in full strength. The Speaker usually recognizes the Leader of the Official Opposition or her or his representative to lead off the questioning. This is followed by the Leaders of the other Opposition parties or their representatives. The Speaker may disallow questions if, in her or his opinion, they are out of order. Members may have another opportunity to pursue a question during what was mentioned earlier as the Adjournment Debate.

If a Member is dissatisfied with the answer to a question asked of a Cabinet Minister, the Member may give notice in writing to the Speaker of her or his intention to raise the matter again, this time during the Adjournment Debate. This notice to the Speaker must be given within one hour after the end of Question Period on the day the question was originally raised.

During the Adjournment Debate, up to five Members may raise matters. Each Member is allowed four minutes to raise the question, and a Cabinet Minister or Parliamentary Secretary is provided with a maximum of two minutes to respond.

## Quorum in the House of Commons

Twenty members of the House, including the Speaker or Chair Occupant, constitute a quorum. If it is brought to the attention of the House that there is no quorum, the Speaker will make an initial count. If there is no quorum, the Speaker shall order the bells to ring for no longer than 15 minutes. A count of the Members present shall then be taken and if a quorum is still lacking, the Speaker will adjourn the House until the next sitting day.

# Chapter 11

# *How A Bill Becomes Law*

One of the most important functions of Parliament is the making of laws. How does the Canadian Parliament carry out this basic responsibility? Parliament makes laws by following rules; that is, by acting within the elaborate framework of its own rules of procedure. As was already mentioned earlier, in the House of Commons, these rules are called "Standing Orders" and in the Senate they are referred to as the "Rules of the Senate."

The purpose of these rules of order is to ensure the orderly transaction of public business while at the same time preserving the basic parliamentary right of freedom of debate. Their function is to control parliamentary discussion in order, as Sir John Bourinot (at one time Clerk of the House of Commons) stated, "to enable every member to express her/his opinion within the limits necessary to preserve decorum and prevent an unnecessary waste of time; and to prevent any legislative action being taken on sudden impulse."

In accordance with these rules of order, all bills—public and private—must pass through various stages before they become law. These stages in the passage of legislation provide Parliament with a number of opportunities to examine and consider all bills, both in principle and in detail, before enacting them into law. They also serve to underline something that is often forgotten: that Parliament, under our Constitution, consists of three elements—the Crown, the Senate, and the House of Commons, each of which has a role to play in the law-making process.

The parliamentary phase of the legislative process is set in motion when a Member of Parliament, that is, a Senator or a Member of the House of Commons, introduces a bill. Once the bill has been debated, has passed through all the legislative stages in both Houses and has received Royal Assent, the process is complete and the bill becomes an Act of Parliament. From that point on, it is referred to as a statute or an Act.

## *Types of Bills*

A bill is a legislative proposal submitted to Parliament for its consideration and approval. Generally there are, basically, two types of bills: public bills and private bills. Public bills are bills that relate to matters of public policy. They deal with such subjects as criminal law, income tax, or unemployment insurance. They may affect the public generally or they may only affect a certain segment of the public. Private bills are bills that confer special powers or rights on a particular person or body of persons. Generally, they are bills to incorporate private companies or religious or charitable organizations or to amend existing acts of incorporation. A private bill is always founded on a petition to Parliament.

There are two kinds of public bills. Those introduced by the Government are called "government bills" and those introduced by private Members are called "private Members' bills" or "private Members' public bills." The government bills take up the greatest amount of parliamentary time. In the House of Commons, private Members' bills can only be considered during the time set aside for Private Members' Business, a daily one-hour period that usually begins at 11:00 a.m. on Monday, 5:30 p.m. on Tuesday, Wednesday and Thursday, and at 1:30 p.m. on Friday. This time limitation, coupled with the complicated procedures that must be followed in order to make a final decision on such bills, explain why very few private Members' public bills are enacted into law.

Bills may be initiated in either the Senate or the House of Commons, although most public bills are introduced in the House of Commons. There are two reasons for this. The first of these is the accountability of the government and individual ministers to that House. The second is the requirement that, under the Constitution, "money bills"—bills involving the appropriation of public funds or the imposition of taxes—must originate in the elected House. Almost all private bills, however, are introduced in the Senate.

## *Legislative Stages*

The "reading" stages are the basic steps in the legislative process. Although a "reading" of a bill does not mean that the bill is actually read aloud to the House. What was once in England an actual reading of a bill is now merely a formality. All bills must pass through the same basic steps in order to become law; however, rules adopted by the House of Commons in early 1994 now provide the House with several options for the order in which a particular bill may pass through the steps in the legislative process. The following is an outline of the basic steps involved in the legislative process. (A brief description of the more modern legislative process options may be found at the conclusion of the section on "Royal Assent.")

*How Parliament Works*

## 1. Notice of Introduction

In the House of Commons, 48 hours' notice is required before a Member can move for leave to introduce a bill. This is done by a notice in writing to the Clerk of the House stating the title of the bill. In the Senate, no such notice is required.

## 2. Introduction and First Reading

In the House of Commons, the first reading of a bill consists of the adoption of three motions. The first is a motion for leave to introduce the bill. The second, which follows immediately, is a motion that the bill be read a first time and printed, and the third is that it be ordered for a second reading at the next sitting of the House. In the case of a Government bill, "the next sitting" means any subsequent sitting on which the Government calls the appropriate order. Although all three motions are purely formal and are not debated, a short explanation of the bill is sometimes given on the motion for leave to introduce the bill.

After the Speaker has declared that the second motion has been carried, a clerk at the Table rises and states "First reading of this bill." Afterwards the bill is sent to be printed. It is normally distributed the next day so that Members may acquaint themselves with its provisions prior to the debate on second reading.

In the Senate, the procedure is much simpler. No motion for first reading is required. A Senator simply rises and says that she or he presents "the following bill," stating its title. The Senator then sends it to the Table and the Clerk Assistant rises and reads the title of the bill, adding "This bill has been read a first time."

## 3. Second Reading

The second reading of a bill is an important stage in a bill's progress through Parliament since it is at this time that the principle of the bill and its broad purposes are fully debated. Debate at this stage can sometimes be lengthy and prolonged.

In the House of Commons, second reading begins with a single motion that the bill "be now read a second time and referred to a committee." In the Senate, there are two motions: one that the bill be read a second time and, when that motion is adopted, a second motion that the bill be referred to a particular committee, if required.

The debate on a motion for second reading begins with an explanation of the bill by the sponsoring Member or Minister. It ends when there are no further speakers or when the sponsoring member rises a second time to speak on the bill.

In the House of Commons, the debate at this and other stages of the bill may also be terminated by a motion of closure or a time allocation motion. In the Senate, there is no provision in the rules for a motion of closure but time limits may be placed on the proceedings through the adoption of a time allocation motion.

A time allocation motion may be moved with or without prior agreement between the government and representatives of the opposition parties to restrict the amount of time to be spent on a bill. The more sparingly used motion of closure in the House of Commons requires no such prior agreement.

4. *Committee Study*

After a bill has been approved in principle at second reading, it is generally referred to a standing committee for detailed consideration. In some cases, however, it may instead be referred to a legislative, special or joint committee, or to Committee of the Whole. The committee may hear as witnesses the Minister or another Member who is sponsoring the bill, as well as departmental or other government officials. It may also hear testimony and receive briefs from interested groups and individuals.

After hearing witnesses, the committee must examine the text of the bill in detail, considering each clause separately, at which time members of the committee may move amendments to any clause. Each clause of the bill, its title, and the preamble (if there is one), is considered and voted upon, with or without amendment, by the committee.

5. *Report Stage*

When the committee has concluded its work, it reports the results of its examination of the bill to the House. Where there are no amendments offered at report stage, a formal motion for concurrence in the bill is made. A motion "That the bill be now read a third time and passed" may then be moved. Should there be amendments proposed, the report stage provides an opportunity to the whole House to adopt or reject the amendments offered by Members, many of whom may not have been members of the committee which studied the bill.

In the House of Commons, forty-eight hours must lapse following the presentation of the committee report before the bill can be considered by the House. During the first twenty-four hours of this time, Members may give notice of amendments they propose to move during the debate at the report stage. If no amendments have been proposed at the report stage, third reading of the bill may be proceeded with immediately. If amendments have been proposed, they are debated at the report stage and a decision is made on the amendments. This is followed by a motion "that the bill (as amended) be concurred in (with further amendments)." If the motion carries, the bill is then ready for third reading at the next sitting.

In the Senate, if a bill is reported without amendment, the report stands adopted (that is, no motion is required for its adoption) and the sponsoring Senator will move that the bill be read a third time on a future day. If the bill is reported with amendments, a debate will take place on a motion to adopt the report. If the motion carries, the bill is ready for third reading.

6. *Third Reading*

The purpose of the third reading is to review a bill in its final form with the changes it may have undergone in its earlier stages. The procedure is similar to that on second reading, the only difference being that, at this later stage, the debate is generally shorter than on second reading.

The third reading motion has a two-fold purpose: (1) the House gives its final approval to the purpose of the bill and (2) the bill itself is approved as the means for achieving its purpose. General argument for or against the bill as a whole is permitted.

A Member may seek to alter the text of the bill at this stage, by moving an amendment to the third reading motion requesting that the bill be sent back to a committee to be amended in accordance with the changes proposed in the motion.

7. *Consideration by Other House*

If a bill has had three readings in the House of Commons, it is sent to the Clerk of the Senate with a message requesting the concurrence of the Senate in the bill. It then goes through the same stages in the Senate as those through which it passed in the House of Commons, with only minor procedural differences. If the bill, on the other hand, originated in the Senate, the order in which it is passed by the two Houses is reversed.

If one House amends a bill passed by the other House, the bill is sent back with a message asking the originating House to concur in the amendments. If that House accepts the amendments, the bill is returned with its concurrence endorsed on the bill. If the amendments are rejected or accepted only in part, the reasons for rejecting them or not accepting them in their entirety will be stated in the message to the House that amended the bill. If that House insists on its amendments, it may inform the other House of this and the bill could potentially be sent back and forth between the Houses a number of times. If the Houses cannot reach an agreement, the bill may not be proceeded with any further. Alternatively, there is provision in the rules for a conference to be held between the two Houses. At this conference, representatives from each House will meet to discuss and, if possible, resolve their differences. If agreement cannot be reached, the bill may be lost. Although such a situation, is extremely rare.

8. *Royal Assent*

When a bill has been passed by both Houses, it is ready for Royal Assent. This is given by the Governor General, in the Queen's name, in a special ceremony held in the Senate Chamber with representatives of both Houses of Parliament in attendance. The Governor General does not usually attend this ceremony in person. Instead, the Governor General is represented by a Deputy, one of the judges of the Supreme Court of Canada appointed by commission for this purpose.

At one point in this historic ceremony, the Clerk Assistant rises and reads, in English and French, the titles of the bills that are awaiting Royal Assent. The Clerk then holds up the bills and says "In Her Majesty's name, the Honourable the Deputy of Her/His Excellency the Governor General doth assent to these bills." The Deputy of the Governor General then signifies assent by a nod of the head. It is this gesture that constitutes "Royal Assent" and it is at this time that the bill is given the force of law, unless there is a provision in the bill stating that the Act or any provision of the Act will come into force on a specific day or on a day to be fixed by order of the Governor in Council.

## New Legislative Process Options, 1994

*A. Committee Prepares and Brings in a Bill*

In this first option, a committee may be ordered to prepare and bring in a bill. In this instance, a Member or Minister, after giving notice, may move a motion to have a committee prepare and bring in a bill. The motion will be debated for up to 90 minutes, after which time it will be put to a vote. If the motion is adopted, the committee will study the matter in question and will submit a report to the House. Depending on who sponsors the motion, a motion to concur in such a committee report will be taken up under either Government Orders or Private Members' Business. If the concurrence motion is adopted, it will be an order of the House to bring in a bill based on the report. When the motion for second reading is proposed, there is no debate; rather, the questions to dispose of the second reading stage are put immediately. If the motion is adopted, the bill will then follow through the remaining steps in the legislative process in the same manner and order as noted in the procedure described above.

*B. Committee Study Before Second Reading*

This second option involves the House referring a government bill to committee for study before it has been read twice by the House; that is, before the House has adopted the bill in principle. This allows the committee to which the bill is referred wider latitude in studying the bill and in proposing amendments.

When the order is called for second reading of a bill, a Minister, after having notified representatives of the other parties, may move that the bill be referred to a committee before second reading. After not more than three hours of debate have occurred, the question will be put to the House. If the motion is adopted, the bill will be referred to committee. The committee will then undertake its detailed study of the bill and thereafter may decide to amend the bill. It will report the bill back to the House. When the report stage and the amendments, if any, have been debated and disposed of, a motion "that the bill (as amended) be concurred in and read a second time" will be proposed. There is no debate on this motion; the House will move immediately to vote on the question. If the motion is adopted, the bill will proceed through the remaining stages in the legislative process as outlined above.

Private bills are passed by Parliament in much the same way as are public bills, although there are some procedural differences. A private bill, for instance, cannot be introduced in Parliament unless the parties who are seeking its passage file a petition with the Clerks of both Houses and pay certain parliamentary fees.

A notice must also be published in the Canada Gazette and in local newspapers and the parties must enlist the support of a Senator and a Member of the House of Commons to act as sponsors of the bill during the various stages of its passage through Parliament.

Private bills may originate in either House. However, since most public bills are introduced in the House of Commons, the practice over the years has been to encourage the introduction of private bills in the Senate as a means of balancing the workload between the two Houses. In fact, petitioners are encouraged to do so through financial and other incentives provided for in the rules of procedure of both Houses.

# Chapter 12

## The Parliamentary Committee System

### Purpose

Committees of the Senate and the House of Commons, in general, perform both investigative and legislative functions.

*1. Investigative*: Committees of both Houses may decide, or be ordered by their respective Houses, to examine a particular subject, e.g. trends in food prices, egg marketing, employee-employer relations in the public service, the estimates, the Constitution, etc.

*2. Legislative*: All bills being examined by the House of Commons are referred to a standing, legislative or other committee for clause-by-clause consideration at some point during the legislative process. The committee may hear as witnesses the Minister and officials of the sponsoring department, as well as interested groups and individuals. After a detailed discussion of the bill, the committee may adopt amendments to the bill. It will then report the bill, with or without amendments, back to the House. In the Senate, the committee examination stage of a bill is optional, and a specific motion sending a bill to committee for study must be adopted by the Senate.

### Types

There are five types of committees: Standing, Legislative, Special, Committee of the Whole and Joint (either standing or special).

Standing committees are permanent in the sense that they are provided for by the Standing Orders or Rules of each House. In the Senate, they remain in existence for the duration of a session; in the House of Commons, they are appointed for a Parliament, but the memberships of the committees will change from session to session and, from time to time, within a session. Standing committees of the House of Commons have three functions: legislative, financial and investigative. They will examine bills as part of the legislative process, undertake ad hoc inquiries and examine estimates and other matters as may be referred to them from time to time by the House.

While many of the standing committees are established to mirror government departments (e.g. Canadian Heritage, Agriculture and Agri-food, Finance, etc.), others have special functions which are not directly related to any particular department (e.g. Public Accounts, Procedure and House Affairs, and Government Operations).

A legislative committee is an ad hoc committee of the House of Commons organized to examine a particular bill. Unlike the procedures followed for standing and special committees, the chairpersons of legislative committees are appointed by the Speaker. Membership on a legislative committee is restricted to a maximum of 15 members.

Special committees are appointed for specific purposes (e.g. to investigate the needs of disabled Canadians, to study constitutional proposals, etc.). Once the particular purpose of a committee has been served and its final report has been presented to the House, it generally ceases to exist.

A Committee of the Whole is established when all of the Members of the House or Senate sit as a committee. The Speaker vacates the Chair and the Deputy Speaker, in the case of the House of Commons, and a Senator selected by the Speaker, in the case of the Senate, presides over the meeting and is seated in the Clerk's chair. In the House of Commons, Committee of the Whole is mostly used for clause-by-clause consideration of bills related to the spending of monies and for non-controversial bills. In the Senate, Committee of the Whole meets primarily to expedite the consideration of financial legislation. Generally, it is used by both Houses when there is a need for speedy passage of legislation.

Joint committees are composed of members of both Houses sitting and working together in matters affecting both Houses. Standing and special committees may be joint committees. Currently, there are Standing Joint Committees on Official Languages, the Library of Parliament and the Scrutiny of Regulations. The mandate of the latter committee is to review and scrutinize subordinate legislation which stands permanently referred to it under the *Statutory Instruments Act.*

## *Composition*

Committees of the House of Commons are composed of members of all political parties represented in proportion to their party strength in that body. When the party in government has a majority in the House of Commons, that political party will have a majority on each committee. If it has a minority in the House of Commons, it will also have a minority in committee. The Chairperson of each committee is usually elected by the committee from among the government members, with the exception of the Chairperson of the Standing Committee on Public Accounts, and the Co-Chair of the Standing Joint Committee on the Scrutiny of Regulations. These Chairpersons are traditionally elected from among the members of the official opposition party represented on the Committee.

The membership of Senate committees is, like the Senate itself, based on equal representation from the four basic geographical regions of Canada. In addition, party representation on Senate committees is in the same proportion as it is in the Senate itself.

## Powers

Committees are "arms" or extensions of the House that establishes them. In each House they have the power to examine, inquire into, and report upon such matters as are listed in the Standing Orders or Rules or as are referred to them from time to time by the House. They are also empowered to call for "persons, papers and records" when required, to administer an oath or affirmation to any witness, and to delegate to sub-committees all or any of their powers, except the power to report to the House. Additionally, a committee has the power to hold a person in contempt of Parliament for refusing to attend as a witness before a committee, if that person was asked to testify. While the committee does not have the power to punish, it may issue a report to the House. The House may then judge what, if any, action may be taken.

In the early 1980s, certain changes to the rules were proposed by the Special Committee on Standing Orders and Procedure and then adopted by the House of Commons. These changes affected the House of Commons standing committees. All reports of government departments, crown corporations, and their subsidiaries, and other agencies laid before the House in accordance with an Act of Parliament are now automatically referred to the appropriate committee. This has significantly extended the scope of a committee's activities. Standing Committees have many powers, including the power to study and report on all matters relating to the mandate, management and operation of the department or departments of Government which are assigned to them. Standing committees also examine matters referred to them by the House. They may send for persons, papers and records and can travel with an order of reference from the House of Commons. Whenever a committee requests, the government must "table" a comprehensive response to a committee report within 150 days of the presentation of that committee report.

In each House, committees activities are often initiated by means of an order of reference from the House. The committee, in interpreting this order of reference, is guided by custom and practice.

## Procedure

The committee, on its own, determines the procedure to be followed in fulfilling its mandate. Custom and practice, however, usually dictate a certain course of events. Prior to the commencement of its deliberations, the steering committee of the larger committee (usually referred to as the sub-committee on agenda and procedure, and composed of the chairperson and a representative of each of the political parties on the committee), will meet and set out a course of action that it will recommend to the full committee.

While the rules of evidence need not be followed, the committee is generally guided by the common law rules of natural justice. When contentious matters arise, witnesses are permitted to have counsel attend with them. The extent of counsel's involvement, however, is determined by the committee. The committee also decides whether it is necessary to swear in a witness. Under the *Criminal Code*, a proceeding before a committee of the Senate or House of Commons is a "judicial proceeding" for the purposes of offences relating to the administration of law and justice.

Article 9 of the *Bill of Rights of 1688* (U.K.) applies both to members of Parliament and to witnesses. Thus, the evidence given by a witness before a committee may not be used in a subsequent civil or criminal proceeding, except in the case of perjury. In the final analysis, the procedure followed in committees represents the collective common sense of the members of the committee.

*An aerial view of Parliament Hill.*

# Chapter 13

## The Parliament Buildings and The Library of Parliament

### The Parliament Buildings

Few Canadians realize that Queen Victoria, in 1857, chose Ottawa as the site of Canada's Capital. She was requested to make this decision after the Canadian Government failed to agree on a site.

Construction began on the Parliament Buildings in 1859 and the Centre Block was ready for its opening on January 8, 1866. At the same time, construction was taking place on two other buildings which today make up the Parliament buildings—the East Block and the West Block. These two buildings were not intended to house the offices of Members of Parliament as they do today, but were constructed to house the entire civil service.

Presently, the East Block remains the only building of the three originally built in 1865 untouched by water or fire damage. The West Block suffered significant fire damage to its top floor in 1897. The Centre Block was supposed to be fireproof when it was built but, in 1916, a fire which started in the reading room, completely destroyed the building, claiming seven lives. Construction to rebuild the Centre Block began soon after and in 1920, a new Centre Block with a new tower was erected.

Today, the Centre Block, easily identified by the Peace Tower, accommodates both Houses of Parliament. After the fire in 1916 destroyed the Centre Block as well as the tower, a new and larger tower was constructed and completed in 1927 to form the entrance of the new Centre Block. It houses the 53-bell carillon, which consists of bells ranging in size from 10 pounds to 22,400 pounds. Visitors to Parliament Hill are able to listen to the recitals from these bells which take place around noon on a daily basis.

*A view of the Library of Parliament and the Marble Statue of Queen Victoria.*

# The Library of Parliament

The Library of Parliament was designed by two architects, Englishman Thomas Fuller and Canadian Chilion Jones, and was opened in 1876. The building reflects the Italian gothic style then in vogue; the exterior has sixteen sides rising to a dome supported by massive flying buttresses. The circular interior, including the two galleries, is panelled with Canadian white pine. The craftsmen diligently handcarved gorgons, crests, masks, and hundreds of rosettes of which no two are exactly alike. The gallery displays eight coats of arms, one for the Dominion, the others representing the seven provinces in 1876. The original floor was an intricate pattern of oak, cherry, walnut, and ash. A white marble statue of Queen Victoria, purchased by the Government from the British sculptor Marshall Wood for two thousand guineas in 1871, stands in the centre. In 1916, the Library escaped the fire which destroyed the rest of Parliament's Centre Block. In 1952, a fire in the dome led to heavy water damage. Renovations permitted the addition of two floors of bookshelves replacing the old stone cellars and the restoration of the rest of the Library.

## *Origin*

The origin of the Library collections dates back to when Canada was divided into two provinces with legislative libraries to be established in Quebec and York (Toronto). The two libraries were amalgamated when Upper and Lower Canada merged in 1841. The first Parliamentary Librarian was appointed in 1856.

## *Mandate*

The mandate of the Library of Parliament is to provide information, research and analysis to Parliament on a non-partisan and confidential basis through the excellence of its staff and information assets. Those entitled to use the services of the Library are the Governor General, members of the Privy Council, Senators, Members of the House of Commons, officers of the Senate and House of Commons, Justices of the Supreme Court of Canada and of the Federal Court, members of the Parliamentary Press Gallery, and other persons with the written authorization from either the Speaker or the Parliamentary Librarian.

## *Services*

The Library staff of over 245 librarians, research officers (including lawyers, economists and political, social, and earth scientists), technicians, and support staff, answer thousands of inquiries and prepare a wide range of research papers. Services include current issue reviews, background papers, bibliographies, abstracts of new books and periodical articles, a bilingual on-line computerized catalogue, access to over 2,500 outside databases, clipping and indexing services, oral briefings, and providing professional staff to assist parliamentary committees and associations.

The Library also provides a video service which consists of taping public affairs broadcasts on video cassettes. The cassettes can be viewed at the Library or can be borrowed by parliamentarians. The Library of Parliament has long been a key element in the Canadian parliamentary life.

*APPENDICES*

# APPENDIX 1

# ELIZABETH THE SECOND

BY THE GRACE OF GOD OF THE UNITED KINGDOM, CANADA
AND HER OTHER REALMS AND TERRITORIES QUEEN,
HEAD OF THE COMMONWEALTH, DEFENDER OF THE FAITH.

TO ALL TO WHOM THESE PRESENTS SHALL COME OR
WHOM THE SAME MAY IN ANYWAY CONCERN

## GREETING:

## A PROCLAMATION

Attorney General of Canada

WHEREAS in the past certain amendments to the Constitution of Canada have been made by the Parliament of the United Kingdom at the request and with the consent of Canada;

AND WHEREAS it is in accord with the status of Canada as an independent state that Canadians be able to amend their Constitution in Canada in all respects;

AND WHEREAS it is desirable to provide in the Constitution of Canada for the recognition of certain fundamental rights and freedoms and to make other amendments to the Constitution;

AND WHEREAS the Parliament of the United Kingdom has therefore, at the request and with the consent of Canada, enacted the Canada Act, which provides for the patriation and amendment of the Constitution of Canada;

AND WHEREAS section 58 of the Constitution Act, 1982, set out in Schedule B to the Canada Act, provides that the Constitution Act, 1982 shall, subject to section 59 thereof, come into force on a day to be fixed by proclamation issued under the Great Seal of Canada:

NOW KNOW You that We, by and with the advice of Our Privy Council for Canada, do by this Our Proclamation, declare that the Constitution Act, 1982 shall, subject to section 59 thereof, come into force on the Seventeenth day of April, in the Year of Our Lord One Thousand Nine Hundred and Eighty-two.

OF ALL WHICH Our Loving Subjects and all others whom these Presents may concern are hereby required to take notice and to govern themselves accordingly.

IN TESTIMONY WHEREOF We have caused these Our Letters to be made Patent and the Great Seal of Canada to be hereunto affixed.

At Our City of Ottawa, this Seventeenth day of April in the Year of Our Lord One Thousand Nine Hundred and Eighty-two and in the Thirty-first Year of Our Reign.

By Her Majesty's Command

Registrar General of Canada

Prime Minister of Canada

GOD SAVE THE QUEEN

# ELIZABETH DEUX

PAR LA GRÂCE de dieu Reine du Royaume-uni, du canada et de ses autres royaumes et territoires, chef du commonwealth, défenseur de la foi,

à tous ceux que les présentes peuvent de quelque manière concerner,

SALUT:

## PROCLAMATION

Le procureur général du Canada

CONSIDÉRANT:

qu'à la demande et avec le consentement du Canada, le Parlement du Royaume-Uni a déjà modifié à plusieurs reprises la Constitution du Canada;

qu'en vertu de leur appartenance à un État souverain, les Canadiens se doivent de détenir tout pouvoir de modifier leur Constitution au Canada;

qu'il est souhaitable d'inscrire dans la Constitution du Canada la reconnaissance d'un certain nombre de libertés et de droits fondamentaux et d'y apporter d'autres modifications:

que le Parlement du Royaume-Uni, à la demande et avec le consentement du Canada, a adopté en conséquence la Loi sur le Canada, qui prévoit le rapatriement de la Constitution canadienne et sa modification;

que l'article 58, figurant à l'annexe B de la Loi sur le Canada, stipule que, sous réserve de l'article 59, la Loi constitutionnelle de 1982 entrera en vigueur à une date fixée par proclamation sous le grand sceau du Canada,

NOUS PROCLAMONS, sur l'avis de Notre Conseil privé pour le Canada, que la Loi constitutionnelle de 1982 entrera en vigueur, sous réserve de l'article 59, le dix-septième jour du mois d'avril en l'an de grâce mil neuf cent quatre-vingt-deux.

NOUS DEMANDONS À Nos loyaux sujets et à toute autre personne concernée de prendre acte de la présente proclamation.

EN FOI DE QUOI, Nous avons rendu les présentes lettres patentes et y avons fait apposer le grand sceau du Canada.

Fait en Notre ville d'Ottawa, ce dix-septième jour du mois d'avril en l'an de grâce mil neuf cent quatre-vingt-deux, le trente et unième de Notre règne.

Par ordre de Sa Majesté

Le registraire général du Canada

Le premier ministre du Canada

**DIEU PROTÈGE LA REINE**

# APPENDIX 2

Whereas Canada is founded upon principles that recognize the supremacy of God and the rule of law:

## Guarantee of Rights and Freedoms

1. The *Canadian Charter of Rights and Freedoms* guarantees the rights and freedoms set out in it subject only to such reasonable limits prescribed by law as can be demonstrably justified in a free and democratic society.

## Fundamental Freedoms

2. Everyone has the following fundamental freedoms: (a) freedom of conscience and religion; (b) freedom of thought, belief, opinion and expression, including freedom of the press and other media of communication; (c) freedom of peaceful assembly; and (d) freedom of association.

## Democratic Rights

3. Every citizen of Canada has the right to vote in an election of members of the House of Commons or of a legislative assembly and to be qualified for membership therein. 4. (1) No House of Commons and no legislative assembly shall continue for longer than five years from the date fixed for the return of the writs at a general election of its members. (2) In time of real or apprehended war, invasion or insurrection, a House of Commons may be continued by Parliament and a legislative assembly may be continued by the legislature beyond five years if such continuation is not opposed by the votes of more than one-third of the members of the House of Commons or the legislative assembly, as the case may be. 5. There shall be a sitting of Parliament and of each legislature at least once every twelve months.

## Mobility Rights

6. (1) Every citizen of Canada has the right to enter, remain in and leave Canada. (2) Every citizen of Canada and every person who has the status of a permanent resident of Canada has the right (a) to move to and take up residence in any province; and (b) to pursue the gaining of a livelihood in any province. (3) The rights specified in subsection (2) are subject to (a) any laws or practices of general application in force in a province other than those that discriminate among persons primarily on the basis of province of present or previous residence; and (b) any laws providing for reasonable residency requirements as a qualification for the receipt of publicly provided social services. (4) Subsections (2) and (3) do not preclude any law, program or activity that has as its object the amelioration in a province of conditions of individuals in that province who are socially or economically disadvantaged if the rate of employment in that province is below the rate of employment in Canada.

## Legal Rights

7. Everyone has the right to life, liberty and security of the person and the right not to be deprived thereof except in accordance with the principles of fundamental justice. 8. Everyone has the right to be secure against unreasonable search or seizure. 9. Everyone has the right not to be arbitrarily detained or imprisoned. 10. Everyone has the right on arrest or detention (a) to be informed promptly of the reasons therefor; (b) to retain and instruct counsel without delay and to be informed of that right; and (c) to have the validity of the detention determined by way of *habeas corpus* and to be released if the detention is not lawful. 11. Any person charged with an offence has the right (a) to be informed without unreasonable delay of the specific offence; (b) to be tried within a reasonable time; (c) not to be compelled to be a witness in proceedings against that person in respect of the offence; (d) to be presumed innocent until proven guilty according to law in a fair and public hearing by an independent and impartial tribunal; (e) not to be denied reasonable bail without just cause; (f) except in the case of an offence under military law tried before a military tribunal, to the benefit of trial by jury where the maximum punishment for the offence is

imprisonment for five years or a more severe punishment; (g) not to be found guilty on account of any act or omission unless, at the time of the act or omission, it constituted an offence under Canadian or international law or was criminal according to the general principles of law recognized by the community of nations; (h) if finally acquitted of the offence, not to be tried for it again and, if finally found guilty and punished for the offence, not to be tried or punished for it again; and (i) if found guilty of the offence and if the punishment for the offence has been varied between the time of commission and the time of sentencing, to the benefit of the lesser punishment. 12. Everyone has the right not to be subjected to any cruel and unusual treatment or punishment. 13. A witness who testifies in any proceedings has the right not to have any incriminating evidence so given used to incriminate that witness in any other proceedings, except in a prosecution for perjury or for the giving of contradictory evidence. 14. A party or witness in any proceedings who does not understand or speak the language in which the proceedings are conducted or who is deaf has the right to the assistance of an interpreter.

## Equality Rights

15. (1) Every individual is equal before and under the law and has the right to the equal protection and equal benefit of the law without discrimination and, in particular, without discrimination based on race, national or ethnic origin, colour, religion, sex, age or mental or physical disability. (2) Subsection (1) does not preclude any law, program or activity that has as its object the amelioration of conditions of disadvantaged individuals or groups including those that are disadvantaged because of race, national or ethnic origin, colour, religion, sex, age or mental or physical disability.

## Official Languages of Canada

16. (1) English and French are the official languages of Canada and have equality of status and equal rights and privileges as to their use in all institutions of the Parliament and government of Canada. (2) English and French are the official languages of New Brunswick and have equality of status and equal rights and privileges as to their use in all institutions of the legislature and government of New Brunswick. (3) Nothing in this Charter limits the authority of Parliament or a legislature to advance the equality of status or use of English and French. 17. (1) Everyone has the right to use English or French in any debates and other proceedings of Parliament. (2) Everyone has the right to use English or French in any debates and other proceedings of the legislature of New Brunswick. 18. (1) The statutes, records and journals of Parliament shall be printed and published in English and French and both language versions are equally authoritative. (2) The statutes, records and journals of the

# DIAN
# OF RIGHTS
# EEDOMS

legislature of New Brunswick shall be printed and published in English and French and both language versions are equally authoritative. 19. (1) Either English or French may be used by any person in, or in any pleading in or process issuing from, any court established by Parliament. (2) Either English or French may be used by any person in, or in any pleading in or process issuing from, any court of New Brunswick. 20. (1) Any member of the public in Canada has the right to communicate with, and to receive available services from, any head or central office of an institution of the Parliament or government of Canada in English or French, and has the same right with respect to any other office of any such institution where (a) there is a significant demand for communications with and services from that office in such language; or (b) due to the nature of the office, it is reasonable that communications with and services from that office be available in both English and French. (2) Any member of the public in New Brunswick has the right to communicate with, and to receive available services from, any office of an institution of the legislature or government of New Brunswick in English or French. 21. Nothing in sections 16 to 20 abrogates or derogates from any right, privilege or obligation with respect to the English and French languages, or either of them, that exists or is continued by virtue of any other provision of the Constitution of Canada. 22. Nothing in sections 16 to 20 abrogates or derogates from any legal or customary right or privilege acquired or enjoyed either before or after the coming into force of this Charter with respect to any language that is not English or French.

## Minority Language Educational Rights

23. (1) Citizens of Canada (a) whose first language learned and still understood is that of the English or French linguistic minority population of the province in which they reside, or (b) who have received their primary school instruction in Canada in English or French and reside in a province where the language in which they received that instruction is the language of the English or French linguistic minority population of the province, have the right to have their children receive primary and secondary school instruction in that language in that province. (2) Citizens of Canada of whom any child has received or is receiving primary or secondary school instruction in English or French in Canada, have the right to have all their children receive primary and secondary school instruction in the same language. (3) The right of citizens of Canada under subsections (1) and (2) to have their children receive primary and secondary school instruction in the language of the English or French linguistic minority population of a province (a) applies wherever in the province the number of children of citizens who have such a right is sufficient to warrant the provision to them out of public funds of minority language instruction; and (b) includes,

where the number of those children so warrants, the right to have them receive that instruction in minority language educational facilities provided out of public funds.

## Enforcement

24. (1) Anyone whose rights or freedoms, as guaranteed by this Charter, have been infringed or denied may apply to a court of competent jurisdiction to obtain such remedy as the court considers appropriate and just in the circumstances. (2) Where, in proceedings under subsection (1), a court concludes that evidence was obtained in a manner that infringed or denied any rights or freedoms guaranteed by this Charter, the evidence shall be excluded if it is established that, having regard to all the circumstances, the admission of it in the proceedings would bring the administration of justice into disrepute.

## General

25. The guarantee in this Charter of certain rights and freedoms shall not be construed so as to abrogate or derogate from any aboriginal, treaty or other rights or freedoms that pertain to the aboriginal peoples of Canada including (a) any rights or freedoms that have been recognized by the Royal Proclamation of October 7, 1763; and (b) any rights or freedoms that may be acquired by the aboriginal peoples of Canada by way of land claims settlement. 26. The guarantee in this Charter of certain rights and freedoms shall not be construed as denying the existence of any other rights or freedoms that exist in Canada. 27. This Charter shall be interpreted in a manner consistent with the preservation and enhancement of the multicultural heritage of Canadians. 28. Notwithstanding anything in this Charter, the rights and freedoms referred to in it are guaranteed equally to male and female persons. 29. Nothing in this Charter abrogates or derogates from any rights or privileges guaranteed by or under the Constitution of Canada in respect of denominational, separate or dissentient schools. 30. A reference in this Charter to a province or to the legislative assembly or legislature of a province shall be deemed to include a reference to the Yukon Territory and the Northwest Territories, or to the appropriate legislative authority thereof, as the case may be. 31. Nothing in this Charter extends the legislative powers of any body or authority.

## Application of Charter

32. (1) This Charter applies (a) to the Parliament and government of Canada in respect of all matters within the authority of Parliament including all matters relating to the Yukon Territory and Northwest Territories; and (b) to the legislature and government of each province in respect of all matters within the authority of the legislature of each province. (2) Notwithstanding subsection (1), section 15 shall not have effect until three years after this section comes into force. 33. (1) Parliament or the legislature of a province may expressly declare in an Act of Parliament or of the legislature, as the case may be, that the Act or a provision thereof shall operate notwithstanding a provision included in section 2 or sections 7 to 15 of this Charter. (2) An Act or a provision of an Act in respect of which a declaration made under this section is in effect shall have such operation as it would have but for the provision of this Charter referred to in the declaration. (3) A declaration made under subsection (1) shall cease to have effect five years after it comes into force or on such earlier date as may be specified in the declaration. (4) Parliament or a legislature of a province may re-enact a declaration made under subsection (1). (5) Subsection (3) applies in respect of a re-enactment made under subsection (4).

## Citation

34. This Part may be cited as the *Canadian Charter of Rights and Freedoms.*

*"We must now establish the basic principles, the basic values and beliefs which hold us together as Canadians so that beyond our regional loyalties there is a way of life and a system of values which make us proud of the country that has given us such freedom and such immeasurable joy."*

P.E. Trudeau 1981

# APPENDIX 3

## *TABLE OF PRECEDENCE FOR CANADA*

1. The Governor General of Canada or the Administrator of the Government of Canada (Notes 1, 2 and 2. 1).
2. The Prime Minister of Canada (Note 3).
3. The Chief Justice of Canada (Note 4).
4. The Speaker of the Senate.
5. The Speaker of the House of Commons.
6. Ambassadors, High Commissioners, Ministers Plenipotentiary (Note 5).
7. Members of the Canadian Ministry:
   (a) Members of the Cabinet; and
   (b) Secretaries of State; with relative precedence within sub-categories (a) and (b) governed by the date of their appointment to the Queen's Privy Council for Canada.
8. The Leader of the Opposition (Subject to Note 3).
9. The Lieutenant-Governor of Ontario;
   The Lieutenant-Governor of Quebec;
   The Lieutenant-Governor of Nova Scotia;
   The Lieutenant-Governor of New Brunswick;
   The Lieutenant-Governor of Manitoba;
   The Lieutenant-Governor of British Columbia;
   The Lieutenant-Governor of Prince Edward Island;
   The Lieutenant-Governor of Saskatchewan;
   The Lieutenant-Governor of Alberta;
   The Lieutenant-Governor of Newfoundland (Note 6).
10. Members of the Queen's Privy Council for Canada, not of the Canadian Ministry, in accordance with the date of their appointment to the Privy Council.
11. Premiers of the Provinces of Canada in the same order as Lieutenant-Governors (Note 6).
12. The Commissioner of the Northwest Territories; The Commissioner of the Yukon Territory.
13. The Government Leader of the Northwest Territories; The Government Leader of the Yukon Territory.
14. Representatives of faith communities (Note 7).
15. Puisne Judges of the Supreme Court of Canada.
16. The Chief Justice and the Associate Chief Justice of the Federal Court of Canada.

*Appendix 3*

17. (a)  Chief Justices of the highest court of each Province and Territory; and

(b)  Chief Justices and Associate Chief Justices of the other superior courts of the Provinces and Territories; with precedence within sub-categories (a) and (b) governed by the date of appointment as Chief Justice.

18. (a)  Judges of the Federal Court of Canada;

(b)  Puisne Judges of the superior courts of the Provinces and Territories;

(c)  the Chief Judge of the Tax Court of Canada;

(d)  the Associate Chief Judge of the Tax Court of Canada; and

(e)  Judges of the Tax Court of Canada, with precedence within each sub-category governed by the date of appointment.

19. Senators of Canada.

20. Members of the House of Commons.

21. Consuls General of countries without diplomatic representation.

22. The Chief of the Defence Staff and the Commissioner of the Royal Canadian Mounted Police (Note 8).

23. Speakers of Legislative Assemblies, within their Province and Territory.

24. Members of Executive Councils, within their Province and Territory.

25. Judges of Provincial and Territorial Courts, within their Province and Territory.

26. Members of Legislative Assemblies, within their Province and Territory.

*Notes*

1. The presence of the Sovereign in Canada does not impair or supersede the authority of the Governor General to perform the functions delegated to her or him under the Letters Patent constituting the office of the Governor General. The Governor General, under all circumstances, should be accorded precedence immediately after the Sovereign.

2. Precedence to be given immediately after the Chief Justice of Canada to former Governors General, with relative precedence among them governed by the date of their leaving office.

2.1 Precedence to be given immediately after the former Governors General to surviving spouses of deceased former Governors General (applicable only where the spouse was married to the Governor General during the latter's term of office), with relative precedence among them governed by the dates on which the deceased former Governors General left office.

3.  Precedence to be given immediately after the surviving spouses of deceased former Governors General referred to in Note 2.1 to former Prime Ministers, with relative precedence among them governed by the dates of their first assumption of office.

4.  Precedence to be given immediately after former Prime Ministers to former Chief Justices of Canada, with relative precedence among them governed by the dates of their appointment as Chief Justice of Canada.

5.  Precedence among Ambassadors and High Commissioners, who rank equally, to be determined by the date of the presentation of their credentials.
    Precedence to be given to Chargés d'Affaires immediately after Ministers Plenipotentiary.

6.  This provision does not apply to such ceremonies and occasion which are of a provincial nature.

7.  The religious dignitaries will be senior Canadian representatives of faith communities having a significant presence in a relevant jurisdiction. The relative precedence of the representatives of faith communities is to be governed by the date of their assumption in their present office, their representatives being given the same relative precedence.

8.  This precedence to be given to the Chief of the Defence Staff and the Commissioner of the Royal Canadian Mounted Police on occasions when they have official functions to perform, otherwise they are to have equal precedence with Deputy Ministers, with their relative position to be determined according to the respective dates of their appointments to office. The relative precedence of Deputy Ministers and other high officials of the public service of Canada is to be determined from time to time by the Minister of Canadian Heritage in consultation with the Prime Minister.

# APPENDIX 4

## *TABLE OF TITLES TO BE USED IN CANADA*

1.  The Governor General of Canada to be styled "Right Honourable" for life and to be styled "His Excellency" and his wife "Her Excellency," or "Her Excellency" and her husband "His Excellency," as the case may be, while in office.

2.  The Lieutenant Governor of a Province to be styled "Honourable" for life and to be styled "His Honour" and his wife "Her Honour," or "Her Honour" and her husband "His Honour," as the case may be, while in office.

3.  The Prime Minister of Canada to be styled "Right Honourable" for life.

4.  The Chief Justice of Canada to be styled "Right Honourable" for life.

5.  Privy Councillors of Canada to be styled "Honourable" for life.

6.  Senators of Canada to be styled "Honourable" for life.

7.  The Speaker of the House of Commons to be styled "Honourable" while in office.

8.  The Commissioner of a Territory to be styled "Honourable" while in office.

9.  Puisne Judges of the Supreme Court of Canada and Judges of the Federal Court and of the Tax Court of Canada as well as the Judges of the undermentioned Courts in the Provinces and Territories:

    Ontario — The Court of Appeal and the Ontario Court of Justice (General Division)

    Quebec — The Court of Appeal and the Superior Court of Quebec

|  |  |
|---|---|
| Nova Scotia — | The Court of Appeal and the Supreme Court of Nova Scotia |
| New Brunswick — | The Court of Appeal and the Court of Queen's Bench of New Brunswick |
| Manitoba — | The Court of Appeal and the Court of Queen's Bench for Manitoba |
| British Columbia — | The Court of Appeal and the Supreme Court of British Columbia |
| Prince Edward Island — | The Supreme Court of Prince Edward Island |
| Saskatchewan — | The Court of Appeal and the Court of Queen's Bench for Saskatchewan |
| Alberta — | The Court of Appeal and the Court of Queen's Bench of Alberta |
| Newfoundland — | The Supreme Court of Newfoundland |
| Northwest Territories — | The Supreme Court of Northwest Territories |
| Yukon Territory — | The Supreme Court of Yukon |

To be Styled "Honourable" while in Office

10. Presidents and Speakers of Legislative Assemblies of the Provinces and Territories to be styled "Honourable" while in office.

11. Members of the Executive Councils of the Provinces and Territories to be styled "Honourable" while in office.

12. Judges of Provincial and Territorial Courts (appointed by the Provincial and Territorial Governments) to be styled "Honourable" while in office.

13. The following are eligible to be granted permission by the Governor General, in the name of Her Majesty The Queen, to retain the title of "Honourable" after they have ceased to hold office:

(a) Speakers of the House of Commons;
(b) Commissioners of Territories;
(c) Judges designated in item 9.

*Appendix 4*

14. The title "Right Honourable" is granted for life to the following eminent Canadians:

-The Right Honourable Martial Asselin
-The Right Honourable Ellen L. Fairclough
-The Right Honourable Francis Alvin George Hamilton
-The Right Honourable Donald F. Mazankowski
-The Right Honourable John Whitney Pickersgill
-The Right Honourable Robert Lorne Stanfield

## APPENDIX 5

## *CANADA'S POLITICAL EVOLUTION*

1864    A meeting of delegates from Nova Scotia, New Brunswick and Prince Edward Island is held in Charlottetown to discuss a union of the Maritime provinces. Sir John A. Macdonald and other delegates from the Province of Canada request permission to attend in order to put forward a proposal for a federal union of British North American colonies.

A second conference to discuss the federal union is held in Quebec City, with representatives from Newfoundland also in attendance. The delegates draft 72 resolutions, which later form the basis of the *British North America (BNA) Act.*

1866    Delegates from Canada, New Brunswick and Nova Scotia meet in London to draft the *BNA Act.*

1867    The *BNA Act* is passed by the Parliament of the United Kingdom. It unites the colonies of Nova Scotia, New Brunswick and Canada (which is divided into the provinces of Ontario and Quebec), and sets out the distribution of powers between the federal Parliament and provincial legislatures. As British legislation, the *BNA Act* can be amended only by the British Parliament, except in very limited areas in which the Canadian parliament is given authority to make changes. Provincial legislatures are authorized to amend their own provincial constitutions, except in regard to the office of lieutenant-governor.

1870    The Province of Manitoba is created by the Parliament of Canada.

1871    British Columbia joins Canada by UK Order in Council.

1873    Prince Edward Island enters the federation by UK Order in Council.

1875    The Supreme Court of Canada is established. However, the Judicial Committee of the Privy Council remains the highest court of appeal. The Canadian Parliament makes provision for a separate administration of the Northwest Territories by passing the *Northwest Territories Act.* The territories are administered from Ottawa until 1967, when Yellowknife is designated as territorial capital.

1878    Substantial modifications are made in the instructions issued to the Governor General, which have the effect of reducing some of his prerogative powers.

1880    Canada posts a High Commissioner to London. The Canadian agent formally participates in international conferences as part of the British delegation.

Great Britain transfers ownership of the Arctic Islands to Canada. This adds about 550,000 square miles to Canada's land area.

1883    At an international conference, Sir Charles Tupper signs protocols on behalf of Canada and apart from the British delegates.

1885    Prime Minister Sir John A. Macdonald refuses to send a military detachment to the Sudan to fight in one of Britain's colonial wars.

1897    At the Imperial Conference, Prime Minister Sir Wilfrid Laurier refuses to consider a proposal for a federation of the British Empire through the establishment of a permanent Imperial Council with the power to determine the tariffs and the military-naval roles of the various colonies.

1898    The Yukon is created as a separate territory with Dawson City as its capital.

1899    Opinion in Canada is divided over the issue of sending forces to assist Britain in the Boer War. Prime Minister Laurier compromises by sending volunteers only.

1905    The Canadian Parliament establishes the provinces of Saskatchewan and Alberta.

1909    At a special Imperial Conference, Prime Minister Laurier declines to contribute to a unified imperial naval command and instead indicates that Canada will build her own navy. In the next year, Laurier introduces the *Naval Bill* to do so.

The Canadian Parliament creates the Department of External Affairs to protect and advance Canadian interests abroad.

*Appendix 5*

1917    On the grounds that Canadians fighting in World War I are militiamen on active service abroad, and thus should remain under Canadian command, the Canadian government establishes its own military headquarters in London and names a Canadian, Sir Arthur Currie, to command the Canadian Corps.

All dominion prime ministers accept an invitation to join with the British War Cabinet in an Imperial War Cabinet.

1919    Canadian representatives take part in the Paris Peace Conference and sign the *Treaty of Versailles*. Canada also becomes a member of the newly-created League of Nations and the International Labour Organization.

1920    Provision is made for a Canadian minister in Washington to be attached to the British embassy.

1922    Prime Minister Mackenzie King refuses aid to Britain in holding a position against the Turks at Chanak.

1923    Canada signs the *Halibut Treaty* with the United States, the first treaty signed by Canada without a British counter-signature.

1924    Canada secures a resolution to modify the League of Nations covenant so that a member of the league is no longer automatically implicated in the actions of other members.

1926    At the Imperial Conference the *Balfour Report* is adopted. It defines the dominions as "autonomous communities" that are "equal in status" and in no way subordinate to Great Britain.

Prime Minister Mackenzie King raises the issue of the Governor General's position at the Imperial Conference, resulting in a formal statement that the Governor General should cease to represent the British government and become the representative of the Sovereign.

1927    Canada's first appointed ambassador is sent to Washington. A dominion-provincial conference is called to find a formula so that full legal power to amend the Constitution of Canada can be transferred from the UK to Canada and thus confirm the status recognized by the

*Balfour Report.* No agreement is reached.

1931   A second dominion-provincial conference is held but an amending formula is not found.

The autonomy of the dominions is given full legal recognition in the *Statute of Westminister.* Because no agreement has been reached on amending formula. Canada requests that the *BNA Act* be excepted from the terms of the statute, and that Britain retain the authority to amend the *BNA Act.*

1935   A third effort to reach agreement on an amending formula is made, again without success.

1937-  The Royal Commission on Dominion-Provincial Relations proposes,
1940   among other things, that responsibility for unemployment insurance be transferred to Parliament.

1939   Canada declares war on Germany one week after Britain has done so.

1940   Responsibilities for unemployment insurance transferred to Parliament by the *BNA Act, 1940.*

1945   Canada is one of the founding members of the United Nations.

1947   The Canadian *Citizenship Act,* the first such act in the Commonwealth, is introduced. For the first time, Canadians are defined as "Canadian citizens" rather than primarily as British subjects born or naturalized in Canada.

1949   Canada is one of the founding members of the North Atlantic Treaty Organization.

Newfoundland joins Canada through enactment by the UK Parliament of the *BNA Act, 1949.*

The Supreme Court becomes the final court of appeal in Canada, ending the role of the Judicial Committee of the UK Privy Council in the interpretation of Canadian constitutional issues.

*Appendix 5*

The Canadian Parliament becomes empowered to amend the Constitution of Canada with respect to "housekeeping matters" at the federal level through the *BNA Act* (No. 2), 1949. Basic areas of the Constitution, including the distribution of powers, still remain within the sole control of the UK Parliament.

1950    The search for an amending formula is renewed at the dominion-provincial conference. No agreement is reached.

1951    Parliament is empowered to legislate respecting old age pensions by the *BNA Act, 1951*.

1952    The first Canadian-born Governor General since Confederation, Vincent Massey is appointed.

1960    Parliament passes the *Canadian Bill of Rights*.

Another effort to find an amending formula results in agreement in principle on the "Fulton-Favreau formula," but subsequently flounders.

1963    The Royal Commission on Bilingualism and Biculturalism is established.

1965    Canada adopts its own flag.

1968-   A series of constitutional conferences, involving a full-scale review
1971    of the Constitution, commences. The outcome of the review is the "Victoria Charter" of 1971, which includes a procedure for patriation, an amending formula and other changes. All first ministers indicate in principle that they will accept the charter, but in the end agreement is not reached.

1969    The *Official Languages Act* is adopted by Parliament.

1975-   Another effort to find an amending formula is initiated, but it is un-
1976    successful.

1978-   The federal government publishes its view on constitutional reform in
1979    a *Time for Action*, and subsequently introduces in Parliament a draft *Constitutional Amendment Bill* (Bill C-60), for discussion purposes.

## Appendix 5

Two First Ministers' Conferences on the Constitution are held with an agenda of 14 items, but no significant agreement is reached.

1979   The Task Force on Canadian Unity, created in 1977 to advise the federal government on unity issues, recommends in its report that there should be a "new and distinctive" Canadian Constitution.

1980   The Canadian Parliament adopts "O Canada" as the national anthem.

The people of Quebec, voting in a referendum, reject sovereignty-association.

Prime Minister Pierre Trudeau and the 10 premiers meet in Ottawa and establish an agenda of 12 items for constitutional negotiations. A committee of federal and provincial ministers is established and the discussions are extended through the summer. The Prime Minister and premiers meet again in September, but fail to reach agreement on any of the 12 items.

The Canadian Minister of Justice introduces a resolution in Parliament for a Joint Address to Her Majesty the Queen, requesting that the United Kingdom Parliament enact provisions for the patriation of the Canadian Constitution, the coming into effect of an amending formula, and the entrenchment of a Charter of Rights and Freedoms and of the principle of equalization.

1981   Following consideration by a Special Joint Committee of the Senate and House of Commons and debates in both houses, many significant amendments to the resolution are adopted.

The legality of the resolution is challenged before the Supreme Court of Canada by some of the provinces. The Supreme Court rules on September 28, 1981, that while the Canadian Parliament can legally act alone, there is a "convention" requiring substantial consent of the provinces.

After further discussions in early November, the Prime Minister and all Premiers except the Premier of Quebec sign an accord on November 5 that breaks the impasse.

In early December the House of Commons and the Senate approve a new resolution which forms the basis of a Joint Address to be sent to London for action.

## Appendix 5

1982    The *Canada Act, 1982* is passed by the British House of Commons and the House of Lords and given Royal Assent by the Queen.

On April 17, in Ottawa, the Queen signs the proclamation, which brings into force the *Constitution Act, 1982*.

1983    At a Constitutional Conference convened by the Prime Minister under section 37 of the *Constitution Act, 1982*, the Prime Minister and nine Premiers agree on a Constitutional Accord on Aboriginal Rights, concurred in by the four national aboriginal associations and both territorial governments.

The Accord includes a Motion for a Resolution to amend the *Constitution Act, 1982*. The amendments deal with provisions for future aboriginal constitutional discussions and aboriginal participation in certain other constitutional conferences, the equal guarantee of existing aboriginal and treaty rights to women and men, and the recognition and protection of rights acquired through land claims agreements.

1984    On June 21, the *Constitution Amendment Proclamation, 1983*, is proclaimed becoming the first "made-in-Canada" amendments under the new amendment formula set out in the *Constitution Act, 1982*.

1987    The last constitutionally mandated First Ministers' Conference on Aboriginal Constitutional Matters is held but participants fail to agree on further constitutional amendments.

1987    Prime Minister Mulroney and the ten Premiers meet at "Meech Lake," a secluded retreat in the Gatineau Hills. The First Ministers agree in principle on a draft document addressing Quebec's five conditions to become a full and active participant in the Canadian federation. This agreement referred to as "The Meech Lake Accord" would also recognize Quebec as a "distinct society" within Canada. After further refining, the Accord was tabled in the House of Commons on June 3,1987 and called for a ratification process by Parliament and all Provincial Legislatures within a three-year deadline.

1990    In June, the three-year deadline for approval by all 10 Provincial Legislatures expires without agreement by all 10 provinces, thus killing the Accord.

*Appendix 5*

The Quebec National Assembly establishes a Commission to examine and make recommendations on the political and constitutional future of Quebec. The Commission is chaired by two Quebec Assembly Members—Michel Belanger and Jean Campeau—and becomes known as the Belanger-Campeau Commission.

In an effort to break a deadlock over the Goods and Services Tax bill, Prime Minister Mulroney employs a previously unused section 26 of the *Constitution Act, 1867* to have eight additional Senators appointed to the Senate. With the additional Senators appointed, the Progressive Conservatives gained a majority in the Senate, and the bill was adopted.

1991    The Belanger-Campeau Commission report concluded that there were only two possible solutions to the constituional impasse between Quebec and the rest of Canada: a profoundly altered federal system or Quebec sovereignty.

1992    The Constitutional Affairs Minister, Joe Clark, meets with all Provincial Premiers except Quebec's. Also invited to the meeting were Aboriginal and Territorial representatives. Tentative agreement is reached on a package which included recognition of Quebec as a "distinct society," the inherent right to Aboriginal self-government and an equal Senate.

Later that summer, the Prime Minister, all provincial Premiers, including Quebec's Premier Bourassa, and Aboriginal and Territorial representatives meet in Charlottetown and unanimously agree to a constitutional package based on their tentative July agreement. This package, referred to as "The Charlottetown Accord," would be put to the people for ratification through a referendum process. The agreement called for two referndums to be held—one in Quebec and one in the rest of Canada. Both referendums were to be held on October 26,1992.

October 26 — The Charlottetown Accord referendums were held and rejected by a majority of both Quebeckers and Canadians outside Quebec.

1993    In February, Prime Minister Mulroney announced his intention to retire and on June 25, 1993 was replaced by Kim Campbell, the newly elected leader of the Progressive Conservative Party. She became Canada's 19th Prime Minister and the first woman to hold that post.

In the October 25, 1993 general election, Jean Chrétien is elected and becomes Canada's 20th Prime Minister.

With this election, the composition of the House of Commons was radically changed. The Progressive Conservative Party, which had governed from 1984-1993, was reduced to two seats, and two previously unrecognized parties, the Bloc Québécois and the Reform Party became officially recognized parties and major players in the House of Commons. Further, the Quebec-based Bloc Québécois, having won one more seat than the Reform Party, became the Official Opposition.

1994    In October, the Parti Québécois is elected to govern Quebec and Premier Jacques Parizeau promises to hold a referendum on sovereignty.

1995    In October, Quebec Premier Jacques Parizeau holds a provincial referendum on the following question: "Do you agree Quebec should become sovereign, after having made a formal offer to Canada for a new economic and political partnership, within the scope of the Bill respecting the future of Quebec, and of the agreement signed on June 12, 1995?"

The referendum question is narrowly defeated by a vote of 50.6% No to 49.4% Yes.

# APPENDIX 6

## *GLOSSARY OF PARLIAMENTARY TERMS*

ACT—a written law enacted by a Legislature, after being debated and approved by the Legislature; also referred to as a statute or enactment.

ADJOURNMENT—the suspension of parliamentary sittings for a limited period of time.

AMENDMENT—a revision or change proposed or made in a law or bill.

ASSENT (ROYAL)—the approval of the Governor General, given to legislation after it is has been passed by both Houses of Parliament.

BILL—a proposed legislative measure submitted to a Legislature for its consideration and approval and, if approved, for enactment with or without amendment, a part of the law of the land.

BILL OF RIGHTS—a formal legislative assertion and declaration of the rights and freedoms deemed to be essential to a group of people (i.e., a nation). Examples:
    The first 10 Amendments to the U.S. Constitution guaranteeing certain rights to the people, such as freedom of speech, assembly, and worship.
    The Act of the British Parliament of 1689 declaring the rights and liberties of the subject and settling the succession to the Crown and declaring that freedom of speech and debates or proceedings in Parliament ought not to be impeached or questioned in any court or place outside of Parliament.

BUDGET—a statement of the probable revenues and expenditures of a country for a fixed period.

CABINET—the committee of Ministers chosen by the Prime Minister and under whose collective leadership the country is governed.

CABINET GOVERNMENT—a government existing according to the principle that collectively the Cabinet must have the support of the majority of Members in the House of Commons to remain in power.

CABINET MINISTER—generally the Senator or elected M.P. chosen by the Prime Minister to be responsible for a particular government department or subject area.

CABINET SOLIDARITY—the principle of solidarity among Ministers of government when facing the opposition or the press.

CAUCUS—a private meeting of members of a parliamentary party; the Members of the House and Senators belonging to a particular party represented in Parliament.

CENSUS—an official enumeration of the people of a nation, conducted in Canada every five years.

CLOSURE—a procedure used by a government to curtail debate on a motion or bill before the House of Commons.

CONFIDENCE OF THE HOUSE—the support voted to a government by the majority of Members of the House of Commons.

CONSTITUENCY—the basic grouping of voters of an electoral district for the purpose of electing an M.P. (another name for a constituency is a riding.)

CONSTITUTION—the document or documents in which the fundamental laws and principles of a country are stated. The Canadian Constitution is defined in the *Constitution Acts, 1867 to 1982.*

CROWN—the monarchal power or regal authority exercised in Canada by the Head of State.

DISSOLUTION—dissolving or putting an end to the term of a certain Parliament.

DIVISION—a recorded vote taken in the House of Commons or Senate.

EXECUTIVE BRANCH—the branch of the government charged with the responsibility for administering the policies to carry out laws adopted by the legislative branch.

FEDERAL SYSTEM—a country where powers are divided between the two levels or orders of government: the federal and the provincial, state or unit governments.

FINANCIAL LEGISLATION—a legislative matter concerning either the raising or expenditures of funds.

GOVERNMENT BILLS—legislative proposals introduced by Cabinet Ministers.

GOVERNMENT ORDERS—items of business sponsored by the government and usually taken up during the time of the House known as Government Orders.

GOVERNOR-IN-COUNCIL—the royal power exercised with the advice of the Cabinet.

HANSARD—the daily verbatim record of the proceedings of the Senate and the House of Commons. Hansard is named after Luke Hansard, the second publisher of British Commons proceedings.

HEAD OF STATE—the Governor General of Canada acting in the name of the Queen as the highest official of the land.

HOUSE OF COMMONS—the elected body of the Canadian Parliament; sometimes referred to as the Lower House.

INDEPENDENT M.P.—an elected member of Parliament who is not aligned or associated with any political party.

JOURNALS OF THE HOUSE—the minutes of the proceedings of the House of Commons, published weekly.

LEGISLATIVE BRANCH—Parliament in its role as a law-making body.

LOBBY—a special interest group trying to influence the way legislators vote on a certain measure.

MINORITY GOVERNMENT—a government which does not have more than one-half of the elected members in the House, and thus must depend on the support of some of the opposition to remain in power.

*Appendix 6*

OFFICIAL OPPOSITION—usually the political party that has the second highest number of seats in the House of Commons.

OPPOSITION PARTIES—all the political parties in the House of Commons except the governing party.

ORDER PAPER AND NOTICE PAPER—the daily agenda of the House, which contains a list of all the items of business that could be considered on a particular sitting day, is the Order Paper; the Notice Paper publication is where the proposals for bills, motions and questions are placed to give the proper notice before introduction or discussion in the House of Commons.

PARTY—a body of persons with similar views on political issues, united with the objective of exercising power through gaining the favour of the electorate.

POLICIES—governing principles or plans that determine courses of action.

PRIME MINISTER—the political leader of the government party.

PRIVATE MEMBER'S BILL—a bill relating to a matter of public policy, introduced by a private Member.

PRIVY COUNCIL—a body established under the Constitution with the general responsibility for assisting and advising the government. It consists of all former and present Cabinet ministers, many former Speakers of both Houses and certain other distinguished persons. The active members are the Ministers of the Crown who are in office and who act as the Cabinet.

PROROGATION—the act by which the Governor General terminates a session of Parliament, the effect of which is to immediately bring to an end virtually all proceedings and business then before Parliament.

READINGS—several of the steps through which a bill must pass before it becomes law.

REDISTRIBUTION—usually after each decennial census, a process which culminates in boundary changes to constituencies. The result may be an increase or decrease in the number of electors in certain ridings, and an increase or decrease in the number of seats in the House of Commons.